GUY MARTIN

PORTRAIT OF A BIKE LEGEND

In memory of my Dad

❝ I get restless. I need a lot going on to keep me occupied and if I didn't have all these things to do, I'd be a very different person and life would be a lot duller. ❞

GUY MARTIN

First published by Carlton Books in 2015
Carlton Books
20 Mortimer Street
London W1T 3JW

Text and design copyright © Carlton Books 2015

Project Editor: Matt Lowing
Editorial: Caroline Curtis, Charlotte Selby and Bronagh Woods
Design: James Pople and Emma Wicks
Picture Research: Paul Langan
Production: Maria Petalidou

A CIP catalogue for this book is available from the British Library.

ISBN 978-1-78097-730-0

10 9 8 7 6 5 4 3 2

Printed in Dubai

FOLLOWING PAGES:
In the zone: Guy Martin preparing for the start of the 2015 Senior TT race.

GUY MARTIN

PORTRAIT OF A BIKE LEGEND

PHIL WAIN

CARLTON
BOOKS

CONTENTS

BORN RACER

Ask anyone in the street who Guy Martin is, and the likelihood is that they'll know. And while some may know him more for his canal boat renovations and record-breaking feats on TV, rather than his results on the track, the fact is, he's helped take motorcycling to a whole new audience. And you have to go a long way back to find a motorcycle racer who's been able to do that.

In 2002, when Guy Martin burst onto the scene, he was one of the most raw, exciting and talented riders in real road racing for more than 20 years. And with his trademark 1960s sideburns, quick wit, unconventional approach and reluctance to embrace the stereotypes of the modern racer, he has firmly established himself as a fan's favourite – and filled a void that the sport desperately needed.

With a penchant for tea, and a thirst for knowledge, the fast-talking Martin was not only different to all other road racers, he was also different to all other 20-year-olds. He was unique, and with his booming laugh, his love for life was clear and helped make him stand out from the crowd.

When Guy was around, people noticed, and his unrivalled enthusiasm, carefree attitude and willingness to always speak his mind meant that he grabbed the attention of whoever happened to be near, whether fellow riders, team bosses or spectators. Combined with his obvious talents as a road racer, this made it clear, even then, that he would be destined to go a long way in the sport.

Since then, he has achieved more than most could ever dream about – both on and off the track – having secured multiple wins and podiums at all of the International road races that take place on public roads around the British Isles, including the North West 200, the Ulster Grand Prix and the world-famous Isle of Man TT Races.

His feats at the TT have almost made him a mythical figure because he's taken a staggering 16 podiums but has still to stand on the top step. With second and third places, lap records, 130mph+ laps, and a high speed crash, his efforts around the legendary Mountain Course are enough to make a film about – which is probably why they did.

The meeting that was arguably the biggest turning point in his career happened on 13-14 July 2002 when the woodland circuit of Oliver's Mount, overlooking the seaside town of Scarborough, played host to the annual Cock o' the North trophy meeting.

The only public road race circuit in England, the Yorkshire venue had assembled its usual array of road racers: some Isle of Man TT and Ulster Grand Prix winners like Ian Lougher and Jason Griffiths, and some clubmen taking their first tentative steps into the real road racing world. But it was Guy who stood out more than most that weekend and made a significant impression on all those that were there.

Martin had been a regular visitor to Oliver's Mount during the 1980s when his father Ian regularly competed, but like all young children he was more used to getting up to mischief in the paddock then. This time was very different. It was the first time he would ever race at the demanding – and dangerous – 2.43-mile circuit. Till then his career, which had begun in 2000, had steered him in the direction of the short circuits and, in particular, the fledgling British Juniorstock Championship, the series that would spawn future British and World Champions, including Tom Sykes, Cal Crutchlow and Tommy Hill.

As we would rapidly learn, young Martin was no respecter of reputations. While it was clear he was riding somewhat loose and with all the carefree enthusiasm of a 20-year-old,

he was also fast and naturally at home on that first weekend, more than keeping up with Lougher, Griffiths and Irish champion Gary Jess. Indeed, he did more than that and ended the weekend with a second place finish in Sunday's 600cc race, beaten only by Jess and ahead of both Griffiths and Lougher.

The leading website of the time, www.realroadracing.com, reported on the event. Welsh maestro Lougher deservedly grabbed the headlines for winning the feature race, but the site also observed that "the meeting also unearthed a potential star of the future in 20-year-old Guy Martin". How right they were.

The irony of Martin's performance was that it was only a last-minute decision that led to him entering the meeting, and racing on the roads certainly wasn't high on his agenda.

Having quickly moved through the clubman's ranks in 2000, Guy had contested the inaugural Juniorstock Championship in 2001. He quickly established himself as a Top 15 finisher, scoring points in eleven of the thirteen rounds to finish eleventh overall, but it's fair to say he wasn't a front runner and didn't set the world alight.

The second half of the campaign was much more positive, however, as he took a best finish of seventh, which gave him plenty of optimism for the following year. Continuing

ABOVE: Guy Martin uniquely competed with a lettered plate, as opposed to a numbered one, in the 2013 Boxing Day road races at Wanganui, New Zealand.

on a GSXR600 Suzuki for a second term in 2002, he built on that end of season form and made great strides forward to become a regular finisher in the Top 6.

A podium finish, at least, looked on the cards at the second round at Brands Hatch, when he led in the early stages ahead of Sykes, Crutchlow and Craig Jones. Then a crash at Graham Hill Bend ended all hopes and an oil spill at the following round at Donington saw the front four riders all crash out although he was at least awarded a fourth-place finish.

He regrouped for the next few rounds and after a couple of solid Top 10 finishes, he ran comfortably inside the Top 5 from the sixth round onwards, climbing back up the Championship table. Fourth place at Snetterton and fifth on the Brands Hatch GP circuit followed, and with a second place to Sykes at Rockingham, he was up to sixth overall.

But Rockingham would prove to be one of the defining moments of Guy's career – and certainly the one that helped steer his career down a different path. Riders had been warned in practice not to run over a white line exiting the chicane coming onto the start and finish – something that he, and others, did during the race. It meant he was given a ten-second penalty and relegated to fifth, something which didn't sit well with the Lincolnshire youngster, who felt the punishment far outweighed the crime.

Storming into race control, he got into a heated argument with a number of the series officials and as he was leaving the office, Race Director Stuart Higgs made an off-the-cuff comment. This was the proverbial straw that broke the camel's back and Martin slammed a laptop lid down on Higgs' fingers.

The result was that Guy, in the space of a few hours, had finished second, been relegated to fifth and then, having contravened a number of regulations in the governing body's manual, told that he had been excluded from the results altogether. It would be three years before he competed in a British Championship meeting again. Nor would this be the last time he clashed with officialdom or became exasperated with politics and bureaucracy within the sport.

The ongoing investigations into the matter meant that, instead of heading to the next British Championship round, he entered the Oliver's Mount meeting. Then, a week later, made his way to Kells in Southern Ireland, where his impact was equally as impressive, in more ways than one.

He recorded his first victories on the roads, winning both the Senior B and Grand Final B races at the world-famous event, but also experienced his first crash, colliding with TT winner and now Rider Liaison Officer Richard Quayle, fortunately without injury. It proved once more that his talent was obvious but also acted as a wake-up call, emphasizing that he needed to rein in his youthful exuberance.

Then came the ruling following the Rockingham incident: just when his fledging road racing career was in the ascendancy, he was banned for six months and now faced an uncertain future. Would his talent for racing between the hedges be snuffed out before it had even got going? Or would he be able to bounce back in 2003?

The rest, as they say, is history. And who knows what would have happened if he hadn't broken the rules on that Sunday afternoon at Rockingham? It was a costly mistake, but one that paved the way for a glittering road racing career to get underway and bring the sport one of its biggest personalities in years. The fact that he's gone a long way outside of the sport too shows just how he appeals to the general public as well as just diehard motorcycle enthusiasts. And his story's certainly got a lot further to run.

1

2002–2003

STARTING OUT

STARTING OUT

With a TT competitor for a father, it's fair to say that racing is in Guy's blood. He was never going to take the conventional path though, and disagreements with officials meant that he was forced to kick-start his career across the Irish Sea. Guy was soon making a name for himself and not even the set-back of a bad crash could stop him from winning his first major title.

Guy was born on 4 November 1981 in Kirmington, a small Lincolnshire village of approximately 300 people. Named after World War 2 pilot Guy Gibson, of Dambusters fame, his was a racing family and as a young boy he travelled with father Ian and mum Rita to the various race circuits up and down the UK.

Even then, he had a penchant for getting his hands dirty and would regularly help (or hinder!) his dad with his preparations. He dabbled in motocross in his teenage years but, by his own admission, he wasn't happy on the dirt and his races would nearly always end in disaster. One such episode led to a trip in the Lincolnshire Air Ambulance, which convinced him he would have to indulge his love of motorbikes in another environment.

Ian Martin had been no mean competitor himself in the 1970s and 1980s, riding a variety of machines and in a variety of championships. He contested the Isle of Man TT Races from 1976 until 1988, his best result coming in 1983 when he finished twelfth in the World Championship Formula One race. When he retired from the sport at the end of the 1988 season, little did he realize that Guy, the second of his four children, would go on to become one of the leading road racers of his generation.

That was all in the future, though, when an 18-year old Guy made his racing debut in 2000. He soon lost his novice jacket as he racked up the results in club meetings at his local Cadwell Park circuit and also further afield at the likes of Mallory Park. The Juniorstock series was tailor-made for a youngster looking to make his mark in front of the British Championship teams and bosses and make a rapid rise up the racing ladder.

That was the logical step for Guy to make next, and that's exactly what he did in 2001 and the early part of 2002 before his career took a significant turn as a result of the Rockingham disqualification. The spat with the BSB organization and ACU governing body led to Guy taking his racing licence from the Motor Cycle Union of Ireland for 2003, something he still races on today, and after six months out of the sport he was raring to go once more. Only this time, he would race in Ireland, contesting a full season of racing, both north and south of the border.

The race meeting where Guy's pure road racing career started, the Cock o' the North Trophy meeting at Oliver's Mount, Scarborough in July 2002.

ABOVE: Bike racing's in the blood: Guy's father Ian in action at Parliament Square during the 1983 Senior Classic Isle of Man TT race

The two road-racing performances he had completed in 2002 obviously hadn't gone unnoticed and he was given an opportunity by an outfit called Team Racing, led by Northern Irish businessman Sam Finlay. All Guy's previous racing efforts had been funded by his Dad's lorry engineering business, where both he and younger brother Stuart worked, and by a number of other local firms, including Bill Banks Haulage.

By no means did Team Racing have a bottomless pit of money, but they were a well-presented outfit, which meant that young Guy could concentrate on the riding. He was still very much hands-on when it came to the preparation of his machines though, as he has been throughout his career.

Due to his lack of racing experience, not just on the roads but also in general – he'd been racing for only 18 months – it was decided that he would not compete in the full Irish Road Race Championships, but rather would contest the Irish short

circuit races and the Senior Support Road Race Championship, a series limited to 750cc capacity machines.

This meant he would be racing on the same circuits as the more established, professional riders such as Adrian Archibald, Ryan Farquhar, Richard Britton and Martin Finnegan, but in a separate race alongside riders at his own level of experience and ability. This also meant he wouldn't take part in the International races, namely the TT, the North West 200 and Ulster Grand Prix.

However, he would be able to tackle the Isle of Man Mountain Course for the first time as he was pencilled in for the Manx Grand Prix, the September event that takes part on the same 37.73-mile course and which is open to amateur riders only. He would also take part in the Southern 100, also held on the Isle of Man, and the races at Oliver's Mount, Scarborough, where he would have additional 600cc and 1000cc machines at his disposal.

ABOVE: Out of the saddle but not of control: Guy at Oliver's Mount, Scarborough, in July 2002.

It soon became clear though that whilst Guy had similar experience to the other riders contesting the Senior Support Championship but much more ability. More often than not, he'd be winning the races by record margins and at a pace that set lap records.

The events of 2002, though, meant that Guy had to build a number of bridges. He arrived in Ireland with a reputation for crashing – a reputation that only intensified on his debut. At a 'closed to club' short circuit meeting at Aghadowey in March, he crashed three times, including once in the pits!

It's fair to say there was an air of discontent surrounding the young Englishman who had come to Ireland to beat the locals. Many felt he was dangerous to ride with, even a liability. However, it was a testament to his personality that, by the end of the season, he had converted just about everyone in the paddock into a Guy Martin fan thanks to his enthusiastic manner and unrivalled will to win. These were traits that would serve him well.

The opening race of the road-racing season in Ireland is traditionally the Cookstown 100, held in April on a 2.1-mile circuit on the outskirts of the town of the same name in County Tyrone. Despite rain falling, Guy opened his account for the year with a devastating win, some 20 seconds clear of his nearest rival. This was achieved despite a near miss at the end of the race when he overshot a corner and had to take a trip up the pavement!

A week later and the Tandragee 100 was the venue, this time on a more challenging and difficult 5.5-mile course – but again it proved no barrier. Grabbing the lead the moment the lights turned green, Guy was never headed to take a four-second win.

As the national season took a break for the North West 200 and TT, Guy was forced to watch from the sidelines. Showing his work ethic and desire to learn, he took up an offer from Martin Finnegan to be his mechanic at the two events. This gave him the opportunity to be involved as much as possible and, crucially, learn as much as possible too. Spending two weeks on the island surrounded by the sport's biggest names would prove invaluable.

Guy's skills with the spanners helped Finnegan, who would become one of his close friends, claim two Top 10 finishes at the TT, but it's fair to say Guy was desperate to get back in the saddle as soon as he could. That came in mid-June at the Dundrod 150 meeting, held on the same high speed 7.4-mile course that hosts August's Ulster Grand Prix.

His demolition of the class continued as he took another emphatic victory, this time by over half a minute – but it was the manner in which he destroyed the opposition that caught the eye, lapping at an amazing 118.391mph, which helped him secure the Championship despite being only halfway through the season. Such were his efforts he would have finished sixth in the feature 600cc race won by Kiwi Bruce Anstey, who would become one of his main rivals in the years ahead.

The success story showed no signs of slowing down when the Championship headed south of the border for the first time and to the Skerries 100. In front of over 30,000 fans Guy took record-breaking victories in both the 750cc and 400cc Support races, demolishing the lap record in the latter by a staggering 7mph. It was clear he was eagerly looking forward to his next two outings – the Cock o' the North at Oliver's Mount and the Southern 100 – where he'd lock horns with the International riders including Lougher, Farquhar and good friend Finnegan.

First up was Oliver's Mount, scene of his memorable debut 12 months previously. This time he was going as a man on a mission and very much as a potential race winner, not an unknown quantity. It's fair to say he didn't disappoint and indeed more than lived up to the hype.

Both days of racing were held in glorious, sunny conditions, ideal for some fast and furious racing. He did exactly that, romping to victory in both of the eight lap legs, which saw him crowned Cock o' the North and claim his first real road-racing trophy. Just for good measure, he also won one of the Superbike races. Although relatively small in stature, Guy was already more at home on the 1000cc Superbikes than the smaller Supersport 600cc machines.

Up until this point in the season, Guy had, aside from the odd low-speed spill, tasted nothing but success. That all changed when he made his debut at the Southern 100 one week later. This would be the first time he'd suffer a high-speed spill and not walk away. It wouldn't be the last.

Martin's wins at Scarborough had given him a feel for the big time. Now the Southern 100, held on a 4.25-mile course near Castletown in the south of the Isle of Man, gave him a second opportunity to pit his wits and talent against the big boys, who were now all too aware of him.

Despite the course being widely recognized as one of the most dangerous of its kind due to its mass starts, narrowness and the close proximity of numerous stone walls, Guy was undaunted and soon got to grips with what was laid out in front of him. He immediately became the fastest newcomer in the history of the event and racked up a whole host of Top 5 finishes prior to the final day's racing and the feature Solo Championship race.

It all went wrong on the opening lap, though, when he missed his braking point at the second corner, Iron Gate, and only narrowly avoided ploughing into the back of Farquhar. Instead, he crashed out on his own, hit the straw bales protecting a stone wall and bounced back into the middle of the road.

Behind him was a full field of 30 machines still to negotiate the corner. Somehow they all managed to miss him – but it was an all too stark reminder of how the sport can bite back. From a high to a low within a matter of minutes, motorcycle road racing isn't for the faint-hearted and puts everyone connected to the sport through all manner of emotions.

His ankle was now pointing the opposite way to where it should have been, and Guy was quickly whisked off to Nobles Hospital by helicopter. He had broken his ankle in several places, the legacy of which can still be seen today.

Even this crash ensured Guy a little piece of fame, though: he was the last person to be operated on at the old Nobles Hospital and the first at the new one only just built! With numerous pins and screws inserted to repair the damage, it put paid to his racing for the rest of the summer months and he was certainly ruled out of the Manx Grand Prix. However, anyone who knows anything about motorbike racers knows that their pain threshold is considerably higher than that of the man in the street, and less than two months later he was back in action.

The ankle was far from healed, and after a tentative outing at Killalane, Co. Dublin on his Dad's BSA Rocket-3, it was a very stiff and sore Guy who lined up at the

" I'm absolutely over the moon... The ankle's been a bit sore this weekend and I've had to soak it in a bucket of cold water in between races, but once on the bike it was alright. This was the one I wanted and I'm made up. **"**

GUY MARTIN ON HIS VICTORY AT THE SCARBOROUGH GOLD CUP IN 2003

International Gold Cup races at Scarborough. With his 1000cc Suzuki slightly modified to aid his comfort on the bike, he was already becoming something of a cult hero at the venue – and he duly delivered.

Before the event, many experts wrote off his chances, due to the injury, but Guy was confident in his own ability. When asked about his prospects, he had no hesitation in informing people he was going to win.

Confidence shouldn't be confused with arrogance and Guy was true to his word. Two wins, two seconds and a third was the outcome from the weekend, and for the first time he added his name to the prestigious trophy, previously won by such illustrious names as Geoff Duke, Phil Read, Giacomo Agostini, Barry Sheene and Carl Fogarty. And all in front of royalty, too: HRH Prince Philip was on hand to present the impressive prize.

"I'm absolutely over the moon," Guy enthused. "The ankle's been a bit sore this weekend and I've had to soak it in a bucket of cold water in between races, but once on the bike it was alright. This was the one I wanted and I'm made up."

It wouldn't be the last time he'd have to ride through the pain barrier, nor would it be the last time his name would be added to the Gold Cup, first awarded back in 1950. With the exertions of the two days leaving him in considerable discomfort and with the main races for the year over, Guy's 2003 season ended on a winning note.

Such a successful season meant that many expected him to remain with Team Racing for 2004 and continue his road-racing education in the feature events. However, despite his tender age, his strong views and single mindedness were already coming to the fore. He was not at ease with the direction the team wanted to take, so he opted to leave and search for a new home. The roads were very much at the top of his agenda now, with first time appearances at the Internationals also a clear priority, and he was, naturally, much sought-after.

He eventually decided to join Uel Duncan Racing, the team set up by the Donegal rider after a crash at the Ulster Grand Prix in 2000 left him paralysed from the waist down. Duncan retained many of the sponsors from his own racing days and this meant he could run a two-man team in 2004. Guy joined established race winner Darran Lindsay in an impressive-looking squad.

A lot had been written about him during the course of the year, some good and some not so good, and mistakes had been made. But what 21-year old hasn't made mistakes? He was ready to admit to them, and also eager to learn so that 2004 would be even more successful. Time was very much on his side although many pointed out that perhaps he needed to adhere to the old adage "you have to learn how to walk before you can run". But even then, they also recognized that this was a rider who was destined to go a long way.

OPPOSITE: Telling a story to Team Racing boss Sam Finlay at the 2003 International Gold Cup at Scarborough. Sister Kate looks a lot more serious.

2

2004–2005

THE REAL DEAL

THE REAL DEAL

A new team, and a step up in racing class, held no fear for the up and coming rider. Guy was soon demonstrating his racing talent, breaking records and showing that he was very much at home on the famous Mountain Course. If other events may have earmarked him as a rider for the future, the 2004 TT definitely confirmed his arrival.

The switch to Uel Duncan Racing was expected to give Guy a platform to develop his career further and to help remove the crasher tag that, perhaps unfairly, was still hanging round his neck. There's an old saying in racing that "you can stop a fast rider crashing but you can't make a slow rider go fast" and this was certainly applicable to him

2004 would prove to be a big year for Guy. The step up in class didn't faze him one bit, in fact he revelled in it, cementing his status as the most exciting talent in road racing for more than a decade.

Duncan provided him with an array of machines that would allow him to contest the Superbike, Supersport and, at the International race meetings, the Production class too. Long-time friend Johnny Ellis - or Trellis, as Guy called him - would be his right-hand man in preparing the bikes and to prove their commitment to the team, they moved camp from Kirmington village to a base in Derry, Northern Ireland for the year ahead.

An awful lot of eyes were watching him closely throughout the year - fellow riders, team managers and spectators - but everyone around Guy, particularly the Duncan team, were keen to remind him that this was another learning year and the next step up to the top echelons of the sport. He had to learn new courses and he went about his trade sensibly and diligently, proving his versatility and also that he was maturing rapidly too.

At the Cookstown 100, he lined up for the opening race of the season. Although he had been promoted to the main National Championships in Ireland, he had to start from the B group at both Cookstown and the following week's race at Tandragee, which ultimately meant he circulated on his own for the majority of the races.

Too quick for the B group, he was not quite quick enough for the front group, and Guy's early season results in Ireland saw him chalk up numerous fifths, sixths and sevenths. The early season national at Scarborough was more profitable. There he was rapidly becoming the dominant figure and he took another hat-trick.

PREVIOUS PAGES: Guy exiting Quarter Bridge on the Robinson Concrete Suzuki during the 2005 Senior TT race. Guy finished third to claim his first TT podium in just his second year around the Mountain Course.

OPPOSITE: A relaxed Guy Martin shares a joke at the 2005 North West 200 with Paul 'Big H' Hunt. Guy's BSB-style hair gel and sunglasses-look didn't last long!

This set him up nicely for his International debut at the North West 200 although his results proved disappointing. This is a circuit he's never fully enjoyed, primarily due to the number of chicanes around the 8.9 miles linking the towns of Portstewart, Portrush and Coleraine, and his best result was a lowly tenth. He was also less than impressed by some of the antics of the 100,000-plus crowd, and he made his feelings plain when he dubbed the event the 'Beer Fest 200'.

This led the doubters to insist that he couldn't cut it at International level. However, others realized that it was too early to judge him and pointed out that the course on the Isle of Man was a lot more suited to his style. What's more, the TT race was also the one where he most wanted to succeed.

His debut around the Mountain Course was eagerly awaited and his performances firmly silenced the remaining critics, finally making them realize what many had been saying all along – that Guy Martin was the real deal.

ABOVE: On the approach to the Gooseneck during the 2004 Production TT. Guy was on course for a Top Ten finish before running out of fuel on the final lap.

One of the topics talked about the most was whether or not he could become the fastest newcomer in the history of the event – first held in 1907 – and perhaps even break the 120-mph barrier. Given that the outright lap record in 2004 stood at 127.29 mph and was held by the late David Jefferies, achieving that would be an almost unbelievable feat.

The previous best lap by a circuit newcomer dated back to 1996, when Jefferies lapped at 115.520 mph on a 600cc Honda in the Senior although that lap was actually bettered by his close friend Ian Hutchinson at the Manx Grand Prix. Hutchinson, who would become a fierce rival of Martin's, showed his potential in 2003 when he won the Newcomers Manx with a lap of 116.66 mph, also on a 600cc Honda.

Guy had the advantage of riding a 1000cc machine for his debut, but that shouldn't detract from what he went on to achieve at that year's TT. If other events had earmarked him as a rider for the future, the 2004 TT definitely confirmed his arrival.

He picked up his pace gradually as the week wore on. He got off to a flyer with twelfth place in the Formula One race, shattering both Jefferies' and Hutchinson's laps with a speed of 120.22 mph. He went quicker still in the Production 1000cc race but was robbed of his first top ten finish when he ran out of fuel on the final lap.

The Junior 600cc and Production 600cc races weren't the most memorable, but the closing Senior most definitely was as he finished in an amazing seventh place. A final lap of 122.10mph made him the fastest newcomer ever and also, at that time, the 29th fastest rider ever around the 37.73 mile course. It was definitely one of the most impressive TT debuts ever and his newcomer's lap stood for three years. When it was broken it took a professional road racer, British Champion and multiple International road race winner in Steve Plater to do it.

One of the most creditable aspects of his performances was that his high start number meant he was circulating on his own for the majority of the races, and so was attaining his results and lap times by himself. The effort he'd put in prior to the event, watching on-board laps on DVD and lapping the course in his van, had certainly paid off. It was evidence of how serious he was about his racing and determination to succeed.

The attention on him was increasing all the time, but Guy was keeping his feet very much on the ground and was content to be learning his trade. He was clearly comfortable living in Ireland and being part of Uel Duncan's team, and his relationship with affable team-mate Lindsay was certainly harmonious. The more established guard were also looking over their shoulders more: TT winners John McGuinness, Adrian Archibald and Ryan Farquhar were all too aware that there was a young upstart rising through the ranks and looking to challenge them sooner rather than later.

Indeed, Guy was out racing somewhere in the British Isles most weekends, and he secured wins in the month of July – once more at Scarborough and, for the first time, at the Southern 100.

He went back to Scarborough for the International Gold Cup meeting, and not only did he retain the trophy won the first time the year before, he won no less than eight of the nine races he started. Only a blown engine in the second Supersport 600cc race denied him an unprecedented clean sweep. For good measure, he also took the outright lap record for the first time, smashing the mark set by Northern Ireland's Phillip McCallen way back in 1994.

To this day, Scarborough is one of the few race circuits he returns to year after year. Speaking after the meeting, he made his affection clear: "Scarborough's where I made my debut on the roads and I love racing there. The weekend couldn't have gone any better and every race went according to plan. The boys did a great job in preparing the bikes, as they have done all season, and I was delighted to retain the Gold Cup. It was especially satisfying to put one over the likes of John and Ryan. It shows that I can beat them and puts me in good stead for next year."

Bold words perhaps, but he was riding a crest of a wave. Though he was still very much in the infancy of his racing career, he'd already shown his speed, intelligence and maturity during 2004. He was learning quickly, both on and off the bike, and certainly looked a lot smoother than the rough-around-the-edges Guy Martin of 2003. If things felt right, he pushed hard – and if they didn't, he took the result and came back stronger next time.

Little wonder that he decided to stay with the same team in 2005. Duncan retained his band of loyal sponsors, which included Gareth Robinson of Robinson Concrete, and a new sponsor, in the shape of Wilson Craig, came on board to back the effort in the Supersport class whilst Barron Transport supplied his Superstock mount. Lindsay remained as team-mate and the only major difference came in the livery of the bikes as they switched from red and blue to a striking red, yellow and black colour scheme.

If a lot was expected of him at the beginning of 2004, then the pressure doubled in 2005. As before, he more than lived up to his billing and delivered the results everywhere he rode. Everyone knew he was talented, but this was the year when he needed to step up and challenge for race wins on a regular basis. And he did.

National race wins and podiums in Ireland came in abundance, his now obligatory victories at Scarborough were taken and, crucially, he stood on an International race podium for the first time, ending the year with three to his name, including a sensational third place in the Senior TT. His overall performance that week was stunning: he finished all five of his races inside the top six, a feat no other rider achieved.

A debut podium looked like it would come in the Superstock race as he lay in third with one lap to go, but a slow pit stop and subsequent 10-second penalty put paid to that. Placing fourth in the second Supersport left him, for once, almost lost for words, having ridden as hard as he thought was possible on the 600cc Honda.

> ❝ **To end the week with five top six finishes from five starts is mint. I was the only rider to achieve that ... and that makes me feel very proud.** ❞

GUY MARTIN ON THE 2005 TT

As it was, it was the final race of the week that gave him that rostrum. Ironically, the Senior saw him go head to head with Martin Finnegan, the rider who had three more years' experience around the Mountain Course and for whom Guy had been mechanic for just two years before. Despite suffering from a sore shoulder – the legacy of a trip over the air fencing at the Mill Road Roundabout during the North West 200 Superstock race – he was able to see off his rival. It was mightily close, though.

The two competitors never saw each other on the track, Finnegan riding at number 4 and Martin number 15 – a fact that also made life difficult for the commentators, who had to wait before confirming the running order. However, a final lap of 126.48 mph made Guy the seventh fastest rider of all time and saw him get the better of Finnegan by just 1.31 seconds after almost two hours of racing. Speaking at the end of the fortnight, he commented:

"I really wanted to take a win this year but realized I wasn't quite ready for it, so to take a podium in only my second year is like a dream come true. I was a little bit disappointed after the second 600cc race, as I thought it would give me my best chance, but the big bike never missed a beat and worked perfectly throughout. My signals kept saying "P3 +0", so I just kept everything as smooth as possible and fate did the rest.

I think I was making up a bit of time through the 32nd, Windy Corner and 33rd as I pushed hard through that section, and to end the week with five top six finishes from five starts is mint. I was the only rider to achieve that and, along with sharing the podium with two great riders like John McGuinness and Ian Lougher, that makes me feel very proud.

Little did he realize that it was a position he'd become very accustomed to between then and now. At the time, though, he was simply over the moon. With just his dad,

OPPOSITE: A fresh-looking Guy in the winner's enclosure after finishing third in the 2005 Senior TT. The grin would be a familiar sight on the podium.

FOLLOWING PAGES: No room for error – Guy exits Kate's Cottage during the 2005 Senior TT with Japanese rider Jun Maeda in hot pursuit.

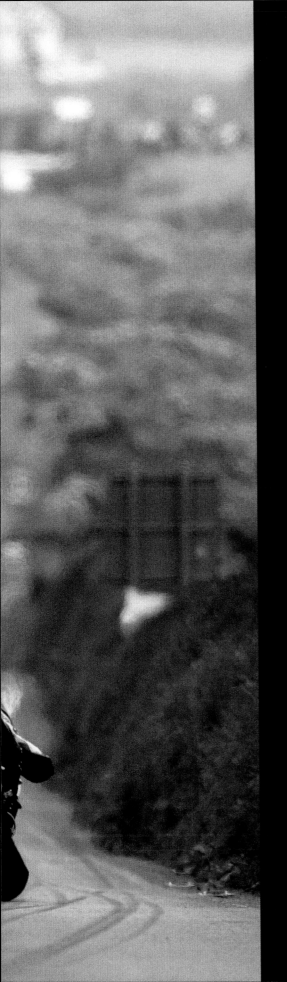

" I really wanted to take a win [the TT] this year but realized I wasn't quite ready for it, so to take a podium in only my second year is like a dream come true. **"**

GUY MARTIN

> ❝ It wasn't the fastest bike out there... That made the results on the island even more satisfying. ❞

GUY MARTIN

Trellis and himself working together, he still maintains that this was one of his most enjoyable and successful years at the TT."

The year's results were particularly impressive because his machines were delayed in arriving in the country and early season meetings at Scarborough and the North West 200 were hit by problems – an experimental breather system at the former nearly denied him a win while damaged radiators and engine blow ups at the latter put him very much on the back foot. A lot of midnight oil was burnt in the days leading up to the TT, but the results would prove he knew how to put a machine together as well as just being able to ride one.

"We had so many problems during practice at the North West, it was unbelievable, and I had to use Darran's Superbike engine from last year for the races. We only finished building it at 1 a.m. on the Saturday morning. It wasn't the fastest bike out there, but it served its purpose although it obviously gave us a lot of work to do prior to the TT. That made the results on the island even more satisfying."

It was back to the National scene after the TT, as he continued to search for his first win in either Northern or Southern Ireland. He didn't have to wait long: victory came in the Grand Final at the Mid Antrim 150 and this set him up for the Ulster Grand Prix, where he was able to add to his collection of International race podiums, two more coming in the Superbike class. Later, looking back, he said:

"After all the seconds and thirds I had, I was beginning to think I'd never win a National race in Ireland and it was particularly pleasing to win at the Mid Antrim, as it's a really tricky course and very demanding on the rider. I had a major moment over Alexander's Jump in practice and it knocked my confidence a bit, so I wasn't expecting that much on race day. But I'd spent a lot of time improving the bike over the previous two weeks and the changes seemed to have

OPPOSITE: Focusing on what lies ahead, Guy gets ready for the Superstock race at the 2005 Ulster Grand Prix. Sister Kate keeps a watching brief.

worked, as the bike was flying. I picked up a few pointers following Ryan during the races and the more the day went on the happier I became.

After the results there, I was confident going into the Ulster and when it was dry I was able to run with the factory riders. When it was wet, track conditions were really tricky and the racing was a bit hairy at times, but I kept focused and rode as hard as I wanted to in the conditions. I had a major moment at Budore in the Superbike race when Ian [Lougher] put a move on me and I ended up on the grass with my feet down and everything. I was determined not to lose any more places and I've got to be happy with two more International podiums."

More wins were taken at Dundalk and Killalane while he had also retained his titles at the Spring National and Cock o' the North meetings at Scarborough. There, he crashed heavily on the Saturday, but he bravely fought back to complete the set with his third successive Gold Cup win. Battered and bruised he showed true grit and determination to take two race wins on the Sunday.

❝ I believe they [Yamaha] will give me the best opportunity of taking a win at the TT, which is my main aim for 2006. ❞

GUY MARTIN

"When I was lying in the road on Saturday afternoon, I never thought it would be possible to race on the Sunday never mind win. It was a big off and I was lucky not to break anything although I was quite dazed. The bike was a fair old mess, but the boys sorted it out whilst I rested as much as I could, although we were lucky the race was delayed at the start, as the front brake was playing up.

We patched it up although we weren't sure it would go the distance. As it was, it got better as the race progressed and although the two Ians, Lougher and Hutchinson, pushed me hard, I was able to edge away in the latter stages."

His season ended with a first visit to November's Macau Grand Prix, the final major International race of the year, where, after struggling to get to grips with the 3.8-mile circuit, he brought the Barron Transport Suzuki home in twelfth place.

By this point, Guy had realized that in order to consistently challenge for International race wins he needed to be with a factory-supported team. So, in early October, he had signed for the AIM Racing Yamaha team funded by wealthy Scottish businessman Alastair Flanagan. Guy was disappointed to leave Duncan's team but positive about the year ahead.

"Leaving Uel's team is an extremely difficult decision, as they're the best thing to have happened to me in racing. I'm sorry to be leaving, but the time felt right to move on and although I had other offers on the table, I feel that the move to Yamaha is the right one for me at this stage of my career. I believe that they will give me the best opportunity of taking a win at the TT, which is my main aim for 2006."

He was due to be joined in the team by triple TT winner and multiple Irish champion Adrian Archibald, who made the shock decision to quit the team before Christmas, which placed doubts both over the team and over Martin's decision to switch camp.

Guy would be on the grid come 2006 though and would complete the season with the team. But in a year that promised plenty, it proved to be a challenging and disappointing season and the first backward step he'd made in his career.

OPPOSITE: Guy on the grid at the 2005 Ulster GP wearing his 'The Carrot Cruncher' decorated helmet.

3

2006

TROUBLE AHEAD

TROUBLE AHEAD

It was a tough decision to move teams but one that Guy knew he had to make if he wanted to challenge the leading riders. Following the switch he would soon be running John McGuinness close at the 2006 Isle of Man TT and leaving spectators exhilarated with a truly imperious display at the Ulster Grand Prix.

John McGuinness had ridden for Alistair Flanagan's team in 2005, taking both the Superbike and Senior TT race victories, but his British Superbike Championship campaign was disappointing and fraught with problems, scoring just 12 points. So it came as little surprise when he moved on at the end of the year, eventually joining the factory Honda team, a position that he still occupies today.

Guy saw plenty of potential in the team, though, because those involved had plenty of experience. Engine tuner Steve Mellor was highly regarded within the racing circle: with Jack Valentine he had been part of the highly successful V&M partnership for more than a decade, winning numerous TT races as well as British Championships. Jim McMahon had been a mechanic for both Honda Britain and TAS Racing, winning International road races also.

The Yamaha R1 and R6 machines were certainly up to the job, as were the Dunlop tyres, and the team would benefit greatly from the direct support of Yamaha UK. On paper at least, it looked like Guy would be in an excellent position to challenge the likes of McGuinness and Lougher at Honda and Bruce Anstey at Suzuki. There would also be a new challenge from the man who'd replaced him in Uel Duncan's team, Australian Cameron Donald.

The change in teams also meant a move away from the National road racing scene in Ireland, as he now took part in selected British Championship rounds instead. The view amongst many was that this was now better preparation for the North West 200 and TT than circuits like Cookstown and Tandragee, primarily due to the extra time a rider had. A BSB rider would get something like four hours of track time over the course of a weekend – and only about a third of that in Ireland.

Guy was happy to race wherever, but he was almost immediately playing catch-up to his rivals as his first outing of the year didn't take place until May's Spring National at Scarborough. By that time, three British Championship rounds had already taken place and he had to wait until July before the results started to pick up.

PREVIOUS PAGES: Guy exiting Rhencullen 2 and beginning the 150mph approach to Alpine Cottage during the 2006 Senior TT. Kiwi Bruce Anstey follows closely.

OPPOSITE: Guy leaves Ballaugh village on the AIM Racing R1 Yamaha during the 2006 Senior TT.

> ❝ **I learnt a lot with the bikes and the Superbike has excellent top speed, as good as anything else out there, and it handles really well.** ❞
>
> *GUY MARTIN*

At the Spring National, his year got off to an inauspicious start at the circuit that had seen him practically unbeatable in the previous three years. May 2006 proved different and he christened his new leathers in the opening Superbike race by crashing out. He remounted to claim fourth, but his mood didn't improve as the combination of a wrong tyre choice and a broken gear lever saw him cross the line in eighth in the second race.

This led to the team withdrawing from the following week's Tandragee 100, and this was far from ideal preparation for the North West 200. Indeed, the rumour mill was in full swing that already, all was not well in the camp. Fuel was then added to the fire when there was no sign of machinery in the race paddock prior to the opening North West 200 practice session on the Tuesday evening. However, the doubters were hushed when the team arrived with a full complement of 2006 machines for the Superbike, Supersport and Superstock races.

As it was, Guy had a good day's racing on the Causeway Coast and although the results didn't quite live up to his usual high expectations he was in the thick of the action throughout. Fourth in the Superstock race would prove to be his best finish of the day, but his mood was certainly brighter than it was when he arrived. He was very matter-of-fact at the end of the day:

"I always want to win, so from that perspective I'm disappointed with the results, but the shortage of track time meant it wasn't really going to happen. A handful of laps around Scarborough compared to BSB rounds and Irish racing is far from ideal preparation. Nevertheless, I learnt a lot with the bikes and the Superbike has

OPPOSITE: Seconds to go – Guy at the start line and awaiting the signal to get his 2006 Senior TT race underway.

excellent top speed, as good as anything else out there, and it handles really well. The North West isn't my favourite circuit either, but I've improved my results and I'm still in one piece and that's the main thing heading into the TT."

The TT couldn't have started any better. He was flying during practice week and after some scorching lap times the decision was made to move him up from number 11 to number 1, the main thinking being that the clear track would be an advantage. Guy later admitted that this probably worked against him, although it was mechanical problems that ultimately wrecked his week.

His impressive lap times in practice had come despite experiencing small oil leaks and it soon came to light that these hadn't been resolved as he only got as far as Sulby on the first lap in the opening Superbike race before the engine blew. Things improved with fourth place in the Superstock, but then took another downturn in the Supersport race when a broken steering damper led to a lengthy pit stop and only 12th place.

A superb opening lap in the closing Senior event placed him just four seconds behind man of the hour John McGuinness, but on the second lap, the oil leak returned, meaning that Guy was battling for survival for the remainder of the race. With considerable bravery, not to mention skill, he manfully continued at speeds close to 200 mph, but with his foot continually slipping off the foot peg. It was no surprise that he eventually dropped back to fifth place. A dejected Guy summed up his week:

"I'm absolutely gutted and am struggling to find the words to sum up how I'm feeling right now. I really thought I could win one this year, but things have gone against us and it was most definitely a case of good practice week, bad race week. The Superbike and Supersport machines were faultless in practice and I'd left myself a bit in reserve where I knew I could push harder in the races if I wanted to, but I never got the chance.

The problems came early on every time and there was nothing I could do. If I'd have pushed any harder, I would have ran the risk of crashing, which you simply can't afford to do round here. It's hard to find any positives, but I was happy with my standing start lap in the Senior and my course knowledge has moved on that bit more. I kept my head up as best I could during race week, so I'll just have to put 2006 down to experience."

The result added further strain to what, from the outside at least, looked like an uncomfortable relationship between Guy and the team. A crash at Scarborough in July didn't help and almost resulted in him missing his favourite Southern 100 meeting but at least he was back on the podium at the latter and slowly beginning to enjoy his racing again.

It was clear he wasn't riding enough, though, and so for the remainder of the year, he competed in the British Supersport Championship, soon becoming a regular in the points. This proved to be a wise decision and when he arrived at August's Ulster Grand Prix, his smiles and laughter were back. Indeed, as we would see in the years to come, the flowing Dundrod circuit allowed him to hit his peak.

OPPOSITE: With the town of Ramsey in the background, Guy peels into Guthrie's Memorial during practice for the 2006 Isle of Man TT races.

To say he was practically unbeatable that week would be an understatement. His performances were simply sensational, and by the Saturday evening, he'd taken four wins and a second from his five starts, to leave the opposition aghast. It was as if a whirlwind had ripped its way through the rest of the field, leaving them to pick up the pieces.

All the races were close and none were handed to him, he had to work hard for them all, but he was ahead when it mattered most and this remains one of the finest days of his career. A day where he could do little wrong and everything went right. Indeed, he was himself a little bit stunned at the end of the day.

"I'm at a bit of a loss to explain what's happened this week and it will probably take a few days to sink in. I've gone from no International wins to having four and everything really has gone perfectly. The races are all a bit of a blur, but although the course was never bone dry, I knew where the damp spots were, so was able to plan accordingly. There's no doubt the short circuit racing has sharpened me up and although it's been a very mediocre season, a good day like today goes a long way to making up for it."

The end of the season was equally successful and he swept the board at the Scarborough Gold Cup, taking seven wins from seven starts. This included his fourth successive Gold Cup victory, making him only the second rider, after Geoff Duke, to win the prestigious

ABOVE: The Southern 100 meeting is Guy's favourite meeting of the year. Here in the 2006 Supersport race, he trails former team-mate Darran Lindsay who would tragically lose his life at Killalane, Ireland later that year.

> ## " If I'd have pushed any harder, I would have ran the risk of crashing, which you simply can't afford to do round here. "
>
> *GUY MARTIN ON THE 2006 TT*

event four times in succession. He also went on to take fifth at Macau, evidence that he was getting to grips with the Far East venue too.

The strong second half of the season led to him agreeing to stay with AIM Racing in October, despite several interesting offers from elsewhere. At this point he intended to contest a full season in the British Championship along with all the major International road races. However, as has often been the case during his career, no contract had actually been signed and just a few months later he announced he was taking up an offer from Hydrex Honda.

Led by former racer Shaun Muir, the team had been in existence for almost 10 years, taking in both the roads and the British Championships, but the Hydrex sponsorship led to them making major strides forward and they were keen to have more of an impact in both, something they duly did. Guy explained his reasons for moving on:

"Everyone assumed I would be staying with AIM and so did I, but things have been up in the air for a while now and I've been speaking to a number of people about 2007. The more I thought about it, the more I thought a change of scenery would do me good. A change is as good as a rest and I just felt like I needed to get a bit more freedom in my racing in order to achieve the goals I've set myself.

Shaun got in touch with an offer and it all went from there. I visited the team headquarters and liked what I saw – Shaun and the guys in the team all speak the same language and tell it as they see it, which suits me fine."

The three Internationals, including the Centennial TT, would be at the top of his agenda along with selected British Superbike rounds, while he'd also get his first taste of the CBR1000RR Honda Superbike on which John McGuinness had been so successful on in 2006. Riding the same bike as the current TT master would put him on an equal footing and prove who the best man really was. There could be no excuses.

4

2007–2008
A LIFELINE

A LIFELINE

Now racing for Hydrex Honda, Guy found himself in a team environment perfectly suited to his needs. The season to come would see improved results on the short circuits and a TT performance that took Guy within a whisker of the top step of the podium.

2006 had seen Guy's career stall somewhat after having made continual progress in the previous three years, so it was obvious that 2007 would be crucial. It was vital that he bounced back, getting back to winning races and being on an International podium. The four wins at the Ulster Grand Prix the previous year had glossed over what had ultimately been a poor season and he couldn't afford a second year of waiting until August for a win. He had to be at the forefront from the very beginning.

For those reasons, the move to Hydrex Honda was initially considered a risk due to the team's lack of road-racing activities. They had last competed at the TT in 2000 with Scot Iain Duffus, establishing themselves in the British Championship paddock in the ensuing years. But Shaun Muir, despite never having raced on the roads himself, had a burning desire to win at the TT – and in Guy Martin, he saw his ideal rider. The win eluded them, but the partnership proved to be an inspired decision by both parties, who had a remarkable season.

The team's infrastructure was as good as anything else out there. Crew chief Mick Shanley was relatively young compared to his peers, but already regarded as one of the best in the business. He'd worked with TT winners Ian Simpson and Jim Moodie in the past as well as spending a number of years in 250cc Grands Prix with Jason Vincent. Guy would certainly have the best support both on and off the track.

Muir put together a package that would see Guy deliver everywhere he raced, and despite the recent inactivity on the roads the whole squad worked brilliantly to establish themselves as a major force between the hedges. Guy also improved considerably on the short circuits, picking up a number of points in the strongest domestic Championship in the world, and by the time he arrived at the North West 200, both man and machine were working well together.

Despite his dislike of the circuit, he was still determined to win and although he didn't quite manage that, he did take his first ever podiums at the venue. Second in the Superbike race behind Steve Plater – who had, ironically, taken his seat at AIM Racing – was his best finish yet, and he backed this up with two thirds in the Superstock and Supersport races. This put him in a great frame of mind going into the Centenary TT: would 2007 be the year he claimed his first win?

PREVIOUS PAGES: Guy's move to Hydrex Honda meant regular appearances on the short circuits in the 2007 British Superbike Championship.

OPPOSITE: The Lincolnshire rider celebrating a podium at the 2007 Isle of Man TT with a cup of tea – the two are never far apart.

" John's the man, though. I said a few things leading up to the races that perhaps I shouldn't and I take my hat off to him for what he did, absolutely awesome. "

GUY MARTIN ON JOHN McGUINNESS

A couple of problems in practice left him parked by the road, but as the Superbike race blasted off, after a number of delays due to the weather, he was immediately inside the top three. Indeed, he was the only rider to get anywhere close to McGuinness. However, as each lap progressed, so too did the Morecambe man's lead and Guy had to accept second. As always, he was big enough to admit the better man had won.

"You always want to win when you take to the line and although I wasn't able to do that today, I gave it my very best shot, and fair play to John. I knew the first lap was going to be crucial, but I was a little bit cautious and didn't quite do as good a job as I could. I spent a little bit too much time behind Ian Lougher just keeping an eye on what he was doing, but I should have steamed past him straightaway. I promised myself I wouldn't be a miserable bugger if I didn't win, and second is a good result to get things underway."

Another podium, in third place, followed in the Supersport race, as well as a new lap record, which just left the Senior – the Blue Riband race of the meeting and the one they all wanted to win. He again pressurised McGuinness more than anyone and though the HM Plant Honda rider would make history by becoming the first man to lap the Mountain Course at more than 130mph, Guy was only four seconds slower. He came agonisingly close to achieving the milestone himself at 129.816mph.

Indeed, television replays would later show that he made a small mistake at Windy Corner and ran wide, and the time lost here was ultimately what cost him. McGuinness increased his lead bit by bit and with a few gearbox problems on the final lap, Guy nursed the machine home for another excellent result.

"I was holding John to two or three seconds in the early part, but I lost a lot of time over the Mountain and really need to pull my finger out at places like the

Waterworks, Tower Bends and the run between the Graham Memorial and the Bungalow, I'm crap at all those places.

Then on the third lap, the chain started to jump the sprocket and the wheel change at the end of the fourth lap failed to resolve it, so I was short shifting everywhere. I didn't think there was any chance of making it home, but we did. John's the man, though. I said a few things leading up to the races that perhaps I shouldn't and I take my hat off to him for what he did, absolutely awesome.

An incident at the North West 200, when Guy overtook McGuinness going into one of the chicanes and forced him down a slip road, led to a few words being exchanged between the two. John later admitted it fired him up, giving him all the ammunition he needed:

"When Guy came steaming by me at the North West, I had nowhere to go other than the slip road. I was spewing at the time, but when I saw it on TV, it didn't look that bad, so I was more annoyed with myself than him. There was a lot of stuff said in the papers about it and I'm not sure about some of the comments Guy made.

He's a character and the sport needs characters and it's not possible to dislike the bloke. He's a bit eccentric and he's very different to the rest of us, but I don't think he's got a bad bone in him. As soon as we got to Snetterton, he came up to me and said, "We haven't fallen out have we, boy?", so we're all friends."

John was not the only rider recognizing that Guy was a likeable character the sport needed, though his comments didn't always win him friends – his dismissal of BSB riders being all hair gel and sunglasses was well known. For Guy, the incident and its fallout was another valuable lesson in his racing education.

After the TT, Guy let his hair down and showed his enthusiasm for all things petrol-driven when he took part in a 12-hour British Lawnmower Association event. He teamed up with brother Stuart and British Superbike team-mate Karl Harris to take on such teams as Northerners Kick Grass and Take it up the Grass. The race was run in torrential rain, there were numerous broken belts and deep mud, and Guy and his team were declared 32nd overall and 16th in class!

With the batteries recharged after a few weeks away from racing, it was soon back to the serious stuff and the Ulster Grand Prix, scene of his incredible five wins the year before. The weather in 2007 meant that a repeat performance was never going to happen, but at a circuit where he was already excelling, he was again the star performer, taking two wins, a second and a fifth from the four races that took place.

The Dundrod 150 Superbike race gave him his first win. He made his move past Ian Hutchinson at the Windmill on the final lap and in a thrilling dash to the chequered flag he managed to hold off TT hero McGuinness by just 0.056 seconds. The overtaking manoeuvre didn't sit well with Hutchinson, and he let Guy know in no uncertain terms what he thought of it after the race but, naturally, Guy saw it differently.

" I woke up to see this Chinese doctor holding me by the waist with one foot against the bed whilst he tried to yank my wrist back into shape. I was still out of it so it took a while for me to realize what was going on. "

GUY MARTIN ON THE 2007 MACAU GP

"Hutchy was riding well and the only place I was quicker than him was through Budore. On the last lap, I got a great run out of Ireland's and lined it up perfectly, pulling alongside him and getting up the inside at the Windmill. He wasn't too happy with me and came up afterwards, saying how I nearly had him through the hedge, but I was nowhere near him.

John McGuinness was right behind us and said it was a fair move. Hutchy would have done the same to me, but the difference would have been that I'd have been the first to congratulate him and say I'd been beaten by the man."

The two riders hadn't seen eye to eye for some time, not aided by the fact that Hutchinson was going out with Guy's youngest sister Kate, but the reality was that both riders were very much on the up and both fighting for the same thing. McGuinness was the top dog in road racing and both Guy and Hutchinson wanted to be seen as the next best thing and the first in line to beat him.

McGuinness commented on the controversy. "Hutchy rode tremendously well for five-and-a-half laps, but I had a feeling something was going to happen. I didn't think Guy would have a go at the Windmill, but he's an opportunist and it was a bit of a 'do or die' move and through he went. It pushed Hutchy a little bit wide and a big door opened for me, which I went straight through! It was an absolutely fantastic race and although Guy's move was a hard one, it was good, clean racing."

OPPOSITE: Guy in action during practice for the 2007 Macau Grand Prix. He was to crash out moments later.

FOLLOWING PAGES: The 2008 British Superbike Championship season gave Guy plenty to think about.

" He's a character and the sport needs characters and it's not possible to dislike the bloke. He's a bit eccentric and he's very different to the rest of us, but I don't think he's got a bad bone in him. As soon as we got to Snetterton, he came up to me and said, "We haven't fallen out have we, boy?", so we're all friends. "

JOHN McGUINNESS ON GUY MARTIN

Guy's final UK outing came, as always, at the Scarborough Gold Cup, which he duly took for a record fifth year in a row, at the same time bettering his own lap record. That just left a third visit to Macau and there his season, quite literally, ended. After his early struggles, he was now completely dialled in with the circuit, so he was very much seen as a potential race winner. During qualifying, he was immediately running in the top four.

It all went wrong in Friday's final session, though, when he crashed heavily, knocking himself out in the frightening-looking spill at a circuit where an unprotected Armco barrier is just a couple of metres away at all times. He was fortunate to get away with concussion and minor breaks in his hands.

"First qualifying went well and it was all going to plan – until I fired it into the wall. On the corner prior to Moorish, I got great drive, probably the best I'd ever got through there, but when I arrived at Moorish I was going that bit quicker than before. I braked in my usual spot, but the extra speed meant I couldn't make it. The last thing I remember is going into the corner thinking 'this is going to be a bit tight' followed by 'I'm not going to make this.'

I was trying hard and made a mistake, so just have to accept it. I hit the wall quite hard and was knocked out for about an hour, so it gave a few of the boys a bit of a fright. I woke up to see this Chinese doctor holding me by the waist with one foot against the bed whilst he tried to yank my wrist back into shape. I was still out of it so it took a while for me to realize what was going on."

Despite the painful end, 2007 was a great year for Guy, so it came as no surprise when he re-signed with Hydrex for the following year. The team had delivered on all aspects, giving Guy the machinery and support they promised, and the partnership had

ABOVE: Guy had a solid season in the 2007 British Superbike Championship and he achieved a lot more track time than in previous seasons.

worked excellently for all parties. With additional sponsorship from Bike Animal, 2008 was expected to be better still.

Once again the three Internationals, Southern 100 and Scarborough meetings would take priority, but he was now full-time in the British Superbike Championship, his first full season in the premier class. John McGuinness and Ian Hutchinson were convinced that the short circuit racing was ideal preparation for the roads, such was the competition now, and Guy had been improving all along, so this was a logical move to make.

In a year that should have given Guy his first TT win, factors conspired against him though and it turned out to be a disastrous year for the now 27-year-old. He suffered all manner of problems both on and off the track, and a series of high profile retirements, most notably at the North West 200 and TT, cost him two Superbike wins.

Guy is very hard himself, but only in the sense that he wants to win every time he goes out on track. Ultimately, that's what separates great sportsman from the merely good. The problems now affected his confidence though and he began to question his own ability. The mechanical breakdowns, as well as a couple of crashes, certainly hurt Guy and he couldn't wait for the season to finish. It did – thanks to a crash, again in Macau.

At the beginning of the new season, though, hopes were high. A delay in the machines and parts arriving in the country meant that very little pre-season testing was done, and the new Honda Fireblade needed considerable work doing to it. Nonetheless Guy scored strongly in the opening rounds of the British Superbike Championship, which included a career best ninth at Thruxton. As a result, he was looking good when he headed to Northern Ireland for the North West 200.

It turned out to be a painful race day, in more ways than one. Brake fade cost him a win in the first Superbike race and left him having to settle for second behind Michael Rutter. It seemed that he'd make amends in the feature Superbike race when he stormed into a three-second lead with just two laps to go. However, a broken radiator hose clip forced him out at University Corner, and for the first time the relationship between the rider and team became stretched.

Guy's day soon got worse: in the second Supersport race he crashed heavily, and spectacularly, at Black Hill, fortunately escaping with just heavy bruising. The crash even made the daily newspapers such was its severity, Guy flying through the air before hitting the grass bank on the outside of the course. Afterwards, he said:

"I'm gutted not to have won at least one of the Superbike races and a double was definitely within my grasp. In the first race, the brakes began to fade at half race distance and I had no way of adjusting them. Dad had made a special bracket for the adjuster, but because of my crash at Brands last weekend, we didn't have time to make a new one. In the second I was just away at the front doing my own thing, but I had a couple of slides and the red light came up on the dash, so I knew it was all over.

It fired me up for the Supersport race, but because we're struggling a bit for top end speed at the moment, I was trying to make up time through all the corners. I went into Black Hill determined to get a good drive along the coast road, but the front end tucked under and it chucked me off. I feel a bit second-hand, but I'll be fit for the TT and although today has been up and down, it's proved I'm as strong as anyone on a Superbike."

ABOVE: Guy was a regular points scorer in the 2008 British Superbike Championship and finished 18th in the overall rankings.

" **I'll be fit for the TT and although today has been up and down, it's proved I'm as strong as anyone on a Superbike.** "

GUY MARTIN ON THE 2008 NORTH WEST 200

Now heading to the TT, Guy didn't do himself, or his relationship with the team, any favours when he competed in the Pre-TT Classic races at Billown. The team didn't even know he was there, and what happened could have put him out of the TT races, the event for which he was being employed. He crashed out after the battery worked its way loose and jammed into the rear wheel. Again, this was a crash that could have had devastating consequences, because he was fired down the road once more. He was fortunate that his injuries were not aggravated further.

Practice for the TT was a lot smoother, although the same couldn't be said for the moments before the opening Superbike race. Back at number 1, Guy was daydreaming somewhere when he should have been on the grid and he lost almost 10 seconds. It was no surprise to see him down in sixth as the times came through from Glen Helen. He gradually got into his stride, though, and an early retirement from McGuinness meant the race was wide open.

By the end of the first lap, he'd taken over in the lead and with his second lap, 129.540 mph, proving to be the fastest of the week, his lead extended to over 10 seconds. Just like the North West 200, though, a probable victory was cruelly taken away from him when, on the approach to Sulby on the fourth lap, a broken crank brought his race to an end.

"I can't even remember what I was doing before the race, but I was arsing about somewhere and I wasn't ready, so I'll hold my hands up for that. One minute I was listening to Rage Against the Machine, the next I was heading down Bray Hill, so I just got stuck in. I was only sixth at Glen Helen, but I don't buy into the thought that you have to be leading there to be in with a chance.

The first two laps went well, I got the fastest lap and got a decent lead, but then the bike just cut out at Sulby on the fourth lap as I changed from fifth gear to sixth – it didn't rattle and it didn't go bang, it just stopped. The crank had broken – no one's fault and just one of those things – shit happens on big jobs.

"An old lady gave me a cup of tea and a can of beer and I got a lift back to the pits in a helicopter, so it could have been worse. As I've said before, racing motorbikes is good, but there's more to life."

GUY MARTIN AFTER THE 2008 SUPERBIKE TT

An old lady gave me a cup of tea and a can of beer and I got a lift back to the pits in a helicopter, so it could have been worse. As I've said before, racing motorbikes is good, but there's more to life."

He bounced back in Monday's Superstock race to claim third, his sixth podium to date, but his bad luck returned in the Supersport race: he only got four miles into the race when the machine expired abruptly. He salvaged a finish with sixth in the second 600cc race, but it was far from ideal, and one of his worst ever years at the TT ended with a generator failure in the Senior, just when he was part of a four-rider dice for the lead.

Looking back, he said, "I was close to tears, I really was. When you put so much effort into something like the TT and build up to it for so long, when it all goes wrong, it's hard to take; it's not like you can put it right the next weekend. It's been 'my year' for the last three years, but I still haven't won and it's beginning to do my head in. I'm sick of hearing it but, thankfully, no one's written me off and we'll keep trying."

With his BSB season going downhill too, the season was unravelling and another retirement, this time due to a front wheel puncture at the Southern 100, saw his mood worsen. Then the Ulster GP was wiped out by the weather, so there was to be no salvage operation for the season there. He did win the Scarborough Gold Cup, becoming the first man to win it six times, but he'd already begun courting a move to Rob McElnea's Yamaha team for 2009.

His nightmare year ended with another crash at Macau. This time, he lasted only four minutes of the very first practice session when he went down at Moorish Corner and was

OPPOSITE: Ignoring the distractions. Guy waits on the grid before the 2008 British Superbike Championship round at Mallory Park.

again knocked out bringing a sorry end to a sorry season. In his own words, it was "the final nail in the coffin of a s*** year".

Nonetheless, Guy remained as the clear fans' favourite for 2009. He was still regarded as the man to challenge John McGuinness and Cameron Donald, the double winner at the 2008 TT. The Australian had already upstaged Guy, which added to his motivation for the new season.

The advanced discussions with Yamaha soured his relationship with the Hydrex team. Curiously, that probably strengthened the resolve of manager Shaun Muir and he gave Guy complete control of his racing affairs in 2009. This meant a step away from the BSB series, where he was never really at ease, and meant that everything was now geared around the TT.

"I said all along that I didn't want to leave Shaun as he's far and away the best person I've worked with, but I just felt certain factors needed to change. I was possibly a bit hasty when I said I was going to leave, but Shaun never wanted me to go and he's done everything to give me the set-up I wanted.

I've got the bikes, the mechanics and race schedule that will suit me down to the ground and whilst it's a shame to leave BSB, I don't think it's the be all and end all that everyone thinks it is and I firmly believe the meetings I'll take in during 2009 will be more beneficial for me. Everything is geared towards the TT, so that's why I'm going to do the meetings I want to do and the ones that will keep a smile on my face."

OPPOSITE: Guy peeling into Braddan Bridge during the Supersport 600cc race at the 2008 Isle of Man TT races.

ABOVE: Guy rounds a tight corner during the 2008 British Superbike Championship season.

5

2009

BACK TO BASICS

BACK TO BASICS

Guy was determined to improve on the previous season, however, his focus on doing so on his own terms risked his relationship with race organisers. Nonetheless, he would be the only rider to achieve three podium finishes at the 2009 Isle of Man TT.

Motorcycle road racing is a tough game, as Guy had learnt in 2008, so it was down to him to put it all behind him and knuckle down to haul himself back to the top. Everything he wanted was in place, from the meetings he would contest to the mechanics he wanted.

The year 2009 also marked the emergence of a new Guy Martin, whose desire to do things his own way, rather than being told what to do and where to go, came to the fore. He had tried doing what everyone else was doing but it hadn't worked for him. He was becoming increasingly exasperated with people telling him what he should and shouldn't have been doing, both on and off the track so, from now on, he was determined to go with his gut instinct.

In a throwback to the old days, Guy simply wanted to turn up and race and not get bogged down with everything else that was required of the modern-day racer. PR and personal appearances weren't for him. His day job as a truck fitter at his dad's yard kept his feet firmly on the ground from Monday to Friday, and racing wasn't the be all and end all. Yes, he wanted to win, but he wanted to do it his way, not the way that everyone else was doing it.

This didn't sit well with some people, particularly race organizers who wanted him to attend promotional events, but they had to become used to it. That wasn't made any easier, however, by the fact that Guy was, arguably, the most popular racer plying his trade on the roads. Everyone was willing him to win, and everyone wanted to see him at the meetings both on the track and in the paddock.

But he was going about his business on his own terms. He was now one of the leading riders, and had sussed out what the game was all about it. Ninety five per cent of the paddock was doing it one way, the remaining five per cent doing it another – and Guy was definitely in the latter group.

His relationship with Mick Shanley was beginning to deteriorate too; a distinct personality clash meant that it just wasn't viable for them to work together anymore. Guy had an "old school" way of riding in that most of what he did on the bike was by

PREVIOUS PAGES: Flying high over Ballaugh Bridge during the 2009 Superbike TT race. Guy was leading by over ten seconds when he was forced to retire on the fourth lap.

OPPOSITE: Braking hard for Governor's Bridge on the 600cc Hydrex Honda during the 2009 Supersport 600cc TT race.

pure feel. He understood exactly how the bike was behaving under him and he would change the settings to suit.

By contrast, Shanley was a whizz when it came to electronics, and the British Superbike Championship was now awash with bikes fitted with the most sophisticated of electronic aids, so he was more used to this analytical path in terms of set-up. Guy didn't want gizmos such as anti-wheelie or traction control on the roads, though, and preferred switching them off completely. Inevitably the relationship between the two men had run its course.

Another factor was that Guy had lost his passion for motorbikes somewhat, and he now believed that a team environment similar to what he'd had in 2005 would help to reignite the flame. Johnny Ellis was brought back into the camp and, with Danny Horne and Cameron "Cammy" Whitworth, the emphasis was on hard work but also

> **❝ The bike is great in straight lines, but not in corners - I've had cracking pit stops, the bike has not missed a beat, so it is down to me and I'm not here to make up the numbers - I wanted the win. ❞**

GUY MARTIN ON THE 2009 SUPERBIKE TT

enjoyment. The bikes were being prepared in his dad's garage too, so everything was being done in-house. His destiny really was, quite literally, in his own hands – only time would tell if this was more beneficial.

Rather than contest one particular championship, Guy still took in a few British Championship meetings but swapped and changed classes, so he was getting time on each bike prior to the road races. He was also being more creative, with innovations such as a custom-made fuel tank for the TT.

Early season outings were more about mileage on the bikes rather than results, but he did take a win at the early season National at Scarborough, bouncing back from a first race spill. This was the result of the larger fuel tank compromising the handling of the bike.

The weather at the North West 200 hindered preparation for the following month's TT: when it wasn't raining, it was blowing a gale. Not one race went the full distance and Guy had a mixed day in terms of both his riding and his results, but that was the same for everyone, and no-one came away any the wiser as to how the form guide was shaping up ahead of the TT.

After a 48-hour delay due to inclement weather, the Superbike TT finally got underway in sunny conditions. As had been the case since 2004, John McGuinness

OPPOSITE: With Kate's Cottage in the background, Guy sweeps round Creg ny Baa in the 2009 Senior TT.

> ## ❝ I couldn't have ridden any harder, so fair play to Hutchy, particularly in the Superstock race, he just rode that bit better than me on the day. ❞
>
> *GUY MARTIN ON IAN HUTCHINSON*

again proved to be unbeatable. He grabbed the lead on the very first lap, and although Guy got to within 10 seconds of him, issues with the set-up of the front forks meant he eventually finished third – more than 50 seconds adrift of the dominant McGuinness.

"The bike is great in straight lines, but not in corners – I've had cracking pit stops, the bike has not missed a beat, so it is down to me and I'm not here to make up the numbers – I wanted the win," he said afterwards.

The second day's racing on the Island saw him claim two hard-fought second places despite having to contend with water getting sprayed onto his visor during the morning's 4-lap Supersport race. There, and in the evening's Superstock encounter, Guy fought tooth and nail with Ian Hutchinson and led both during the course of the 150.92 miles.

The Supersport race saw the water issue force him back to third, but a final lap inside the old class lap record saw him reclaim second. In the Superstock race, it truly looked like he'd claim his first win when he opened up a three-second lead over Hutchinson at half-race distance. However, the Yorkshire rider was in inspired form and with a new lap record of almost 130mph, he overturned his deficit and converted it into a near nine-second win.

"I couldn't have ridden any harder, so fair play to Hutchy, particularly in the Superstock race, he just rode that bit better than me on the day. I was a bit slow on the first run to Glen Helen and gave myself a bit of work to do. I managed to get in the lead, but my signals kept saying '+0' and although I caught some backmarkers in some awkward places on the last lap, Hutchy had the same. So no excuses."

Team boss Muir was also happy with how the week was going. "Guy's taken two more podiums today and has broken both of the class lap records, so we can't complain too much and certainly can't fault anything. The approach and endeavour

❝ It's been a mixed TT, but I was the only rider to take three podium finishes, so that's something to be pleased about, I guess. **❞**

OPPOSITE: MotoGP
legend Valentino Rossi
dishes out the plaudits
on the 2009 Superstock
TT podium.

ABOVE: Guy tunes
into some music as
he prepares for
another TT race.

FOLLOWING PAGES:
After years of trying,
Guy finally won the
Southern 100 Solo
Championship race in
2009, here shown just
before Joey's Gate.

has been first class and with three podiums from three races, I've never seen Guy's confidence so high."

Everyone in the team was buzzing, but it turned out that this would be a week of two halves. The three podiums were swiftly followed by two retirements, an overheating engine forcing him out of the second Supersport race and a broken chain as he left the pits to start lap five eliminating him from the Senior. In what was rapidly becoming a recurring theme, it was very much a case of what might have been.

"I had a scare at the beginning of the Senior when the bike wouldn't start and we'd swapped to a new set of forks, so it took me a while to get going. I worked my way up to third, but when I put the bike into gear after the second pit stop, the chain broke clean off, another one of those problems that we could have done nothing about. It's been a mixed TT, but I was the only rider to take three podium finishes, so that's something to be pleased about, I guess."

> **" I love the Southern 100, it's my favourite meeting of the year ... after all the second places over the years, it's mint to finally win the main Championship race. "**
>
> *GUY MARTIN*

Guy had courted controversy during the TT fortnight by working away from the traditional pit area, preferring instead to base himself and the team a few miles away in a rented garage. It was the first sign that Guy and the TT organizers weren't seeing eye to eye, and although they came to a compromise, it was clear that appearances at signings, chat shows and radio interviews during the fortnight would soon become a thing of the past.

With his race week ending on a low note, Guy returned to the truck yard, where the transport manager helped console him with some homemade vodka. He then returned to the farm of his then girlfriend Kate, mowing the lawn to earn his keep, but he was soon downbeat again after a number of their mountain bikes were stolen. Mountain biking was a pastime that had rapidly become one of Guy's major interests, and he had begun entering endurance competitions.

A plan to take in July's Mega Avalanche, a downhill mountain bike marathon event in Austria, had to be shelved because of the loss of his bikes. Instead he headed off to Maribor, Slovenia to watch the fifth round of the Mountain Bike World Cup and have a bit of a break before his racing resumed in July.

When it did, it was at the Southern 100. After years of trying, which included three successive runner-up spots, he finally got to add his name to the list of Solo Champions. It was close, though, and he only got the better of Ryan Farquhar by one-tenth of a second after a thrilling contest throughout the nine laps.

"I love the Southern 100, it's my favourite meeting of the year and after all the second places over the years, it's mint to finally win the main Championship race. It wasn't easy, though, and all of the Superbike races were flat-out, but I managed to just hold Ryan off. He was riding really well and had got the better of me twice earlier in the week, so it was nice to turn the tables on him."

Farquhar had taken four wins from four starts prior to the main Championship race and during the race it took him longer than he would have liked to have got past Michael Dunlop, which allowed Guy to edge away.

"In the first two Superbike races," Farquhar said later, "I'd managed to get by Guy each time on the final lap, firstly at Castletown Corner and then at Cross Four Ways, but in the main Championship race, he took the lead early on and pulled away. Once I'd got by Michael, I was able to reel him in and it all came down to the last lap, but a backmarker got in the way slightly on the final corner. I'm pleased with second, though, and it's been enjoyable racing with Guy all week."

After some time away from the Irish Championships, Guy enjoyed solid performances at both Kells and Armoy, which both saw unusual occurrences. Race fans at Kells saw him competing in the unusual helmet colours of Adrian Archibald after his own AGV model sustained damage from flying stones at the Southern 100 just days earlier. At Armoy, he had a rare outing on a 250cc.

Armoy was the latest addition to the Irish calendar and it instantly became a favourite of Guy's. It is one of the few meetings he still takes part in, primarily to build up to the Ulster Grand Prix. "The course is absolutely mega, one of the best I've ridden, and it has without doubt the fastest corner in road racing – quicker than Gorse Lea at the TT, quicker than Budore at the Ulster, quicker than anywhere. I'd go as far to say it's one of the manliest courses on the calendar!"

The preparation for that year's Ulster GP duly worked. Although he had to wait until the final race of the day, after taking numerous leaderboard positions, he ended the meeting with victory in the final Superbike race with less than half a second separating Guy, Gary Johnson, Conor Cummins and Ian Hutchinson.

A seventh consecutive Gold Cup win at Scarborough followed, although he admitted it was his hardest yet as Hutchinson pushed him all the way. We didn't know it at the time, but this would be his final outing with Hydrex Honda. After three years with the team – mainly successful ones, at that – Guy would move elsewhere for 2010. He was continuing to look for the missing ingredient that would give him a much yearned-for TT win.

His season wasn't totally over, though. A return to Macau wasn't possible (the meeting was by invitation only and organizers had a ruling that too many crashes would disqualify a rider), but he did head overseas, this time for the Kings of Wanneroo event, held at the Barbagello Raceway on the outskirts of Perth, Australia.

Organized by *Irish Racer* magazine and the Western Australia motorcycle club, this saw a host of British riders including World Superbike star Jonathan Rea, Ryan Farquhar, Conor Cummins and Guy take on a number of Australian riders over three races.

Many saw it as an opportunity to let their hair down, and whilst that certainly was the case – Farquhar shaved off one of Guy's trademark sideburns after a drunken night out – the racing was taken seriously and the Brits issued a heavy defeat to the locals.

The internet forums were awash with rumours that Guy had already signed for TAS Racing, but when the new year came, it was announced that he'd be riding for Wilson Craig Racing. He had first encountered the Northern Irish businessman when racing for Uel Duncan's team back in 2005.

6

2010
CLOSE TO THE EDGE

CLOSE TO THE EDGE

The 2010 season saw Guy Martin join Wilson Craig Racing and it proved to be the most eventful yet. The year would see the Lincolnshire rider have a major run-in with race authorities and survive a 170mph crash on the Mountain Course.

Martin and Wilson Craig had remained firm friends over the years and with Craig's own team having flourished with Scotsman Keith Amor, the duo got talking. A deal was subsequently agreed with Guy's traditional handshake. He would remain on Honda machinery but would have control over everything, a step further down the line from what he'd had in his final year with Hydrex.

The individual nature of Guy would come out more during 2010 as he tried to go back to basics as much as he could. If he had his own way, he'd have turned up to every meeting and worked out the back of a transit van, but while that wasn't possible, his set-up was a lot smaller than the fancy articulated trucks and awnings of the likes of TAS Racing and HM Plant Honda.

It also meant that he wouldn't appear at any of the press days hosted by the Isle of Man TT and North West 200 because he'd decided the best way forward was to concentrate on his riding. Chat shows weren't going to help him in his quest for victory at the TT, working on the bikes would.

"It really annoys me," he said later, "when I read and hear people slagging my way of working off, saying I'm doing it all wrong and that. I might not have won a TT last year, but I was the only person to get 3 podiums at the TT, I won at the Southern 100, I won at the Ulster and I won at Scarborough. So, overall, we did quite a bit and I think it proved my way does work. It just needed a bit more fine-tuning, which, hopefully, has now been done."

The back to basics attitude sat well with many. Others scoffed at the fact that on the one hand he wanted to work out of the back of a van, and on the other he had just purchased an Aston Martin worth well over £100,000. Some of his critics were beginning to see him as a nearly man who was constantly contradicting himself and trying to be different to anyone else.

This argument would continue to run and there was a degree of truth to it. Only a degree though; it was more a case of Guy continually searching for the best package, environment and set-up that would give him the best chance of success.

PREVIOUS PAGES: Guy negotiates Sulby Bridge on his way to another second place, this time in the 2010 Supersport 600cc race.

OPPOSITE: Within touching distance. Race fans are always close to the action at the TT as this 2010 picture at Hillberry shows, with Guy just a few feet away.

The "different" tag gained further weight, though, when his colour scheme for the year was revealed. A plain silver bike with the rider clad in plain black leathers was a throwback to the 1960s, when racing was a lot simpler. Guy's explanation was that he simply wanted to race in the colours of one of his Dad's favourite road bikes, a 1999 VFR800 that celebrated 50 years of Honda motorbikes.

Whatever the reason, it certainly stood out from the rest in their bright, corporate colours, but race wins would still come down to who was the fastest rider, not the colour in which their bike was painted.

It turned out to be a fraught beginning to the year for Guy, who quickly found out that things weren't quite going how he wanted. The North West 200 was a disaster, clutch problems with his Superbike were accompanied by a series of blown engines for the 600. Craig also had a relationship with Simon Buckmaster's Parkalgar Racing team, which didn't sit well with Guy. He was also not happy about certain aspects of their preparation of the 600cc Honda, and he quickly decided he would have to have all the bikes based in Kirmington.

"I'm an extremely meticulous person when it comes to my work," he explained, "and am very particular in how I like things to be done. I like my bike to be prepared in a certain way and if it's not, then I'm not going to ride it. I need confidence in what I'm throwing my leg over. So, after the North West, we brought the Superbike and 600 back to Kirmington, stripped them down and got them 100% ready for the TT."

ABOVE: Guy about to negotiate Tower Bends during practice for the 2010 Isle of Man TT races. He is riding the Wilson Craig Racing Honda Superbike.

Unbeknown to many, Guy was also featuring heavily in a British documentary film about to be released. *TT 3D: Closer to the Edge* would introduce the sport – and Guy – to millions who had never before been aware of the TT. Indeed, it became the seventh-highest-grossing documentary in the UK of all time and would change Guy's life, giving him amazing opportunities.

When he arrived at the TT, Guy already seemed to be wound tighter than the proverbial coil – off the track at least. When he was out on the bikes in practice, he could do what he does best: ride well and ride fast. As expected, he was on the leaderboard in all of the classes and came into race week as a potential race winner in all five solo races.

The opening Superbike race saw local hero Conor Cummins take an early lead with a stunning opening lap just fractions of a second outside the outright lap record. Ian Hutchinson was in second and Guy in third, and the positions were still the same at two-thirds race distance.

But upon leaving the pits after his second pit stop at the end of the fourth lap, Guy received a 30-second penalty for exceeding the pit lane speed limit of 60 km/h. The ruling had been brought in for the 2010 meeting to slow riders down and prevent accidents with riders having to adhere to this limit from the top to the bottom of pit lane. Numerous riders fell foul of the ruling and received a penalty but Guy was the highest profile one.

His speed was only 0.112 km/h over, but the rules were the rules and he dropped down to fifth. Cummins retired shortly afterwards, which meant that without the penalty Guy would have been second to race winner Hutchinson by just over 16 seconds. Instead, he finished fourth. This led to numerous arguments with the race officials, but the penalty, and result, stood.

"I wasn't happy about it," he admitted later. "I just can't believe there was no tolerance. Engineers have a tolerance, police have a tolerance with speed guns, etc, so I just thought it was incredibly harsh. It really wound me up, not on the bike, but with the whole organization side of things. I can't be doing with press conferences and just don't want to be involved with that, so I decided to be awkward and do things when I wanted to and in my time, not when other people told me too."

A titanic 600cc race followed on the Monday morning with Guy locked in battle with arch-rival Hutchinson. The two were riding similar 600cc Hondas, and there was nothing between them throughout the four laps, but it was the Padgetts-prepared machine of the Yorkshire rider that came out on top by just three seconds. Guy was second again and, still seething from Saturday's penalty, he courted controversy when he first refused to go to the winner's enclosure and then left the podium early.

"There are no excuses from me in that 600cc race. I finished second by three seconds and Hutchy beat me fair and square. I don't think I was disrespectful to him or Michael (Dunlop) on the podium, as I clapped them and shook their hands, saying well done – I told Hutchy he'd ridden brilliantly. It was the organizers that I was angry with and it was only because of Wilson and the boys that I went to the podium and press conference – they deserved to see me there."

The evening's Superstock race was a whole different story. On the very first lap, Guy had a major slide at Appledene, which he attributed to cold tyres. His first pit board told

> **❝ I'm extremely meticulous when it comes to my work ... I like my bike to be prepared in a certain way and if it's not, then I'm not going to ride it. ❞**
>
> *GUY MARTIN*

him something he didn't want to see – P11. As always, he pushed as hard as he could and despite a few more unsettling slides, he fought his way up to fifth.

The second 600 was a similar story with more front end slides, including a monumental one at Glen Moor filling station when he ran over his foot. Admitting later that he simply didn't want to push any harder, he nevertheless finished in a strong fourth, which left just the Senior race for his last chance of a race win.

It had been a tumultuous week, but his determination was like never before and he took off like the proverbial scolded cat. An opening lap of 131.108 mph put him second, although it was mightily close: just 3.6 seconds covered McGuinness, Guy, Hutchinson and Cummins. McGuinness still led on the second lap, but his advantage over Guy was just 0.91 seconds. Hutchinson was only two seconds adrift in third.

The riders duly took their first pit stop – and just minutes afterwards, disaster struck. The worst thing possible at the TT is hearing the words "Red flag – the race has been stopped." This generally means that an accident has occurred on the circuit, and when an accident requires the race or practice session to be stopped, it's serious – or worse.

There are a number of notorious black spots around the TT course, and while many corners have claimed lives, some are particularly notorious for proving fatal. One of these is Ballagarey – or Ballascarey as the riders call it. If you come off there, there is normally just one result – death. Kenny Blake, Phil Hogg, Colin Gable and Mike Casey had all been killed there in the 1980s and 1990s, and just a day before the Senior, New Zealander Paul Dobbs had also paid the ultimate price. Crash at Ballagarey, and the chances are you won't be walking away from it.

OPPOSITE: A rear wheel landing for Guy at Ballaugh Bridge in 2010.

There was silence all over the Island when the race was stopped. Everyone quickly realized that Guy was involved when he failed to appear at Glen Helen. And when further announcements said that the accident had taken place at Ballagarey and that a fire engine was on the course, everyone feared the worse.

Guy had gone into the corner at close to 170 mph and had lost the front end, hitting the straw bales protecting a solid stone wall on the outside of the circuit. A full tank of fuel after the pit stop meant that a huge fireball erupted, both the bales and a hedge catching fire. The bike had flown through the air as Guy tumbled down, and across, the road, eventually coming to a halt almost 500 yards later.

Riders behind had to negotiate what they described as a bomb scene and it felt like an eternity before the commentary team announced that Guy was conscious and that his injuries weren't life-threatening. To survive a crash at Ballagarey was one thing, to avoid sustaining serious injuries was another.

Two factors had probably saved Guy– his undoubted skill and the fact that he came off halfway round the corner rather than on entry. Despite everything happening in milliseconds, his instincts told him he was in trouble, so he tried to save the bike from crashing for as long as possible. By hanging on to the bike, he'd got further round the corner and although the impact was still huge, he was able to ricochet off the protective bales as opposed to going straight into them. That made the difference. Reflecting on the crash later, he said:

"I tried to hang on to the bike for as long as I could. I've no idea what happened, as I wasn't doing anything different to all the other laps I'd been through there. Same peel-in point, same line, everything. Before the race, we'd changed a couple of things but nothing major at all, just a bit of extra foam on the seat and half a click on the suspension. But I knew I'd lost it as soon as I went in. The glass is always half full for me, though, and I'm the eternal optimist, so when the front tucked, I was adamant I was going to get it back.

ABOVE: With his camel pack providing pre-race fluid, Guy walks to the grid at the 2010 Isle of Man TT races.

OPPOSITE: Completely airborne at Union Mills during an evening practice session at the 2010 Isle of Man TT.

I held it and held it and then thought I'm not getting this back and that's when I opted to fall off the side and let the bike take the impact in the bales, which is when the tank exploded. I followed it in, then got fired across the other side to hit the wall on the right and then slid about 400 yards down the middle of the road."

An amateur photographer caught the immediate aftermath of the crash on camera. To say the fireball was huge is an understatement, the petrol tank clearly being seen some 30 feet in the air. The end result for Guy was six broken ribs, two punctures in his right lung, four chipped vertebrae, two broken vertebrae and a twisted knee. His protective Dainese leathers did an amazing job, but the friction caused him to lose some skin whilst his hair and eyebrows were also singed from the fire.

"A lot of people have been asking me since the crash if it's going to change me and I've answered the same every time – not one little bit. I have appreciated things a lot more since the accident, though, and I am aware it was a big crash. I think the fact I saved it for as long as I could, rather than sliding at 90° into a wall, helped and someone was definitely looking after me."

After the crash, Guy was in hospital for, amazingly, less than a week. He pencilled in July's Southern 100 for his comeback meeting, but the doctors refused to sign him off as fit for racing. Besides, it soon became apparent this wasn't going to be possible. The recovery progress was slow and he admitted that mowing the lawn put him out of action for about three days!

"I got up on the Monday morning to go to work," he explained, "and pretty much collapsed at the side of the bed. It's not the sort of pain where you can grit your teeth and get through it. It's the type of pain that renders you useless and in absolute agony. I'll come back when I'm 100%, so maybe the Ulster is a more realistic goal."

ABOVE: Guy sweeps round Douglas Road Corner, Kirk Michael during the 2010 Superbike TT race.

> **"** It's not the sort of pain where you can grit your teeth and get through it. It's the type of pain that renders you useless and in absolute agony. **"**

GUY MARTIN

August's Ulster GP was indeed the scene of his return to racing, just over two months after his big TT get-off. The high-speed Dundrod circuit, the fastest in the world, has always been one of Guy's favourites and although he didn't win, or indeed get on the podium, his return was considered a success. He finished all five of his races inside the top six and challenged for the rostrum places in each.

"Initially, I thought I'd only race the 600, as I didn't think I'd be strong enough to hold on to the big bikes, but I chucked them in the van and we decided to give it a go and see where we ended up. I was fine through all the high-speed, one direction corners like Deer's Leap or Budore, but I was struggling when I was having to constantly change direction at high speed, particularly from the hairpin to the start and finish where it's all left-right, left-right.

The Ulster really made me realize how much you use your legs and knees to steer the bike and the amount of upper body strength you need to muscle the bike around. I'm man enough to admit I wasn't quite 100%, but I went out there and gave it a go. I couldn't have tried any harder, that's for sure."

His only other outing of the year came at Scarborough where he saw his run of success in the Gold Cup come to an end. He failed to start the wet race, a lack of spare tyres meaning he pulled in after the warm-up lap.

The year had obviously been hugely interrupted by the TT crash, but the move to Craig's team and "back to basics" approach hadn't reaped the rewards Guy had hoped for. It was a time for a re-think.

So, 2011 saw him move to pastures new, his fifth team in seven years. This time, he went to the opposite end of the spectrum as he joined one of the biggest teams in the paddock – TAS Racing. It was also one of the most successful.

7

2011–2012
A NEW BEGINNING

NO HALF MEASURES
ENERGY · STAMINA · FOCUS · DRIVE

A NEW BEGINNING

Guy took centre stage for his new team as TAS Suzuki's sole rider in 2011. He rewarded them with a number of strong performances but came under increasing pressure from critics who suggested his work away from the track was impacting his racing.

Martin signed for the TAS Suzuki team, backed by energy drink Relentless, in November 2010, citing their unrivalled success and family run environment as the two most important factors. He would also be their sole rider – unlike previous years where, in common with the other leading teams, they'd fielded two.

Run by father and son Hector and Philip Neill, and based in Northern Ireland, the team had racked up 14 TT wins since 2002. Hector also had more than 30 years of involvement within the sport, having previously been involved with the late, great Joey Dunlop and Norman Brown. Bruce Anstey and Cameron Donald left the team at the end of 2010, paving the way for Martin to be signed. He explained:

"I've been talking to Philip for a few years now. Last year was an up and down season for me and I ended up doing too much with the team. Instead of thinking what I was doing on the bike, I was thinking about where the lads would be staying at the next meeting, what parts needed to be ordered – all that kind of stuff. My head was going at a million miles per hour and I'll admit, I wasn't really in the right frame of mind to be racing.

When Philip rang and made me an offer, it got me thinking. And the more I thought about it, the more it made sense. They've won everything going and the experience they have can only be beneficial to me. When someone says they've wanted to work with you for a long time, it fills you with confidence and the whole team knows what they're doing."

"It's been a difficult decision changing our line-up as we pride ourselves on loyalty," added Neill. "In saying that, Guy is a rider I've wanted to work with for a couple of seasons now, and my loyalty to other riders probably held that decision back a little. He came to us full of enthusiasm and wants to do things our way, which was a good starting point. And on top of that, I'm a sucker for a challenge and I like Guy's free spirit attitude. He's created a Guy Martin brand without even trying and that's also pretty special."

PREVIOUS PAGES: Guy exits York Corner at the 2011 North West 200 road races.

OPPOSITE: An intense-looking Guy prepares for a meeting in 2011.

The North West 200 meeting was all but wiped out by a combination of bad weather, an extensive oil spill on track and a bomb hoax. Only a solitary 600cc race was held, – which meant that Guy missed out on valuable set-up time prior to the TT. Although he'd competed at his usual Scarborough and Cookstown meetings, there was plenty of work to be done on the trio of GSXR Suzukis.

He didn't get off to a great start, either, in the opening Superbike race. He was running in the Top 3 for the majority of the early laps, but it all came to an end for Guy near Hillberry on the fifth lap when generator failure caused the 1000cc machine to grind to a halt. As is often the case, the TV cameras caught it all as Guy parked the bike next to a gate and trudged disconsolately into a field to gather his thoughts.

"That was a disappointing end to what looked like a certain second place, but that's the TT for you. We got off to a great start and were well within striking distance of John on that opening lap. From there I just kept it steady and felt pretty comfortable. After the second stop I knew John was going to be near impossible to catch, but you gotta keep trying, and we were well in control in second place. I was looking around the dash frantically trying to see what had gone wrong and when I got to Keppel Gate I knew the job was... well you know the rest."

However, from there on in it was nothing but success for Guy, who finished all four of his remaining races on the podium. Third place was the outcome in each of the Supersport races, as well as the Superstock encounter, but the Senior was ultimately his best moment of the week. Indeed, it would prove to be one of his best ever rides on the island as he went head to head with John McGuinness for the entire six laps.

It was Guy that set the early pace and, with an opening lap of 131.038 mph, he opened up an impressive five-second gap on the Padgetts Honda of Bruce Anstey, with

ABOVE: A rare short circuit outing in 2011 since Guy chose to focus on road race events in that year.

OPPOSITE: Guy takes some time out before the start of a practice session at the 2011 Isle of Man TT.

McGuinness following. He continued to lead when the riders came in for the first round of pit stops at the end of lap two, but McGuinness was ominously eating into his advantage, gaining further ground in the pits, his squad having had plenty of practice in their World Endurance championship campaign.

Towards the end of lap three, McGuinness got the advantage he sought, and it was one he wouldn't relinquish. Guy had to re-focus his efforts on repelling Anstey, who had closed to within two seconds. Up front, McGuinness, the soon to be 17-time TT winner, settled into his familiar front-running position, steadily opening up a gap. Anstey briefly took over second place, but Guy was back ahead as they went out onto their fifth lap.

The final lap saw McGuinness hold a lead of 13.2 seconds and although Guy cut the deficit with a last ditch effort, he had to again accept second, this time by 7.2 seconds. Both riders were inside the old race record and it remains the quickest and fastest six laps Guy has ever done around the Mountain Course.

"I can't remember being pushed that hard in a Superbike race for a very long time," said McGuinness. "It took me a lap or so to get into the rhythm of the Superbike again and I made the odd little mistake at the beginning. Guy was away with it but I settled down after lap two, we had a mega pit stop and after that I was just going for it. I was pushing really, really hard but after another good pit stop, I could breathe a little and hold enough of a pace to stop Guy catching me. He made me work for it, though!"

It was Guy's sixth second place finish, and thirteenth podium finish – meaning that he now shared with Jason Griffiths the unenviable record of taking the most TT finishes without a win. Guy would have to wait three more years before getting back on to the podium, but at the time, he could only acknowledge and admire McGuinness' exploits.

> **❝ I'm a sucker for a challenge and I like Guy's free spirit attitude. He's created a Guy Martin brand without even trying and that's also pretty special. ❞**
>
> *PHILIP NEILL*

OPPOSITE: Guy leads his regular race sparring partner Ryan Farquhar through Joey's Gate at the 2011 Southern 100.

FOLLOWING PAGES: Guy exiting Tower Bends during the 2011 Isle of Man TT with fellow Lincolnshire rider Gary Johnson chasing.

"What can I say, he's my hero!" he said afterwards. "I did absolutely everything I could and couldn't have wished for a better start. Those first two laps were mint but John's a wily old bugger and he gradually reeled me in. The bike was faultless and I gave it my all, but the better man won, it's as simple as that."

Self-effacing in defeat as always, Martin had nonetheless fully vindicated his decision to join the team at the beginning of the season: four podiums from four finishes was a superb return on the Suzuki machinery. It seemed that, finally, he'd found his spiritual home, one that would allow him to flourish. The smile was certainly back, and it's fair to say Guy was enjoying racing, and life, again.

The family atmosphere suited Guy down to the ground. The Relentless by TAS Suzuki team had barely seen a change in personnel over the previous ten years, and it was a happy one. As the saying goes, a happy rider is a fast rider – and in 2011, Guy was both.

He had to give way to Michael Dunlop at the Southern 100 after a typically hard-fought race, but another International victory came his way at the Ulster GP, when he clinched the final Superbike race of the day. His name was back on the Scarborough Gold Cup too and no-one was surprised when he re-signed for the team for the following 2012 season.

"My view is that if it's not broke, then don't fix it, so that's why I've stayed with TAS. Hector and Philip [Neill] 'get' me. Hector's a great bloke and Philip knows how to get the best out of me. He knows I don't like all the PR stuff, but he gets me to do what I need to do. It's brilliant. I'd trust my mechanics – Mark, Denver and Danny – with anything and whilst I've a bit of a thing when it comes to doing stuff with the media or having cable ties on my bike the boys fill me with confidence."

The team was rebranded in new livery for 2012, the security company Tyco coming on board as title sponsor, and Guy found himself with a team-mate again in the shape of Manxman Conor Cummins. The duo had become good friends on their trip to Australia at the end of 2009 and the talented youngster would be a formidable opponent.

Guy made his first appearance of the season at the Cookstown 100 and following that, it was straight on to the North West 200. It again proved to be a painful experience though as he crashed heavily at Dhu Varren in Saturday's opening Supersport race causing it to be red flagged. The GSXR600 was completely written off in the high-speed spill. Fortunately, and despite hitting the kerb hard, the only damage to him was mild concussion and bruising.

Given the nature of his injuries, Neill withdrew Guy from the remainder of the meeting, but this led to rumours of a "bust-up" between the duo, the rumblings continuing when they arrived at the Isle of Man. Interviewed on Manx Radio, Hector Neill dismissed the rumours as nothing more than "media inspired skullduggery, paddock tittle-tattle and unfounded hear-say."

However, just like 2008, Guy risked incurring the wrath of his team when he contested the Pre-TT Classic races at Billown. The meeting almost ended in disaster for him, and he was lucky to escape further injury when he crashed on the final lap of the Superbike race. Understandably, this led to further reports of tension between himself and the Tyco team.

Guy was now regularly being asked the million-dollar question: Why hadn't he won a TT? He'd been upstaged by numerous riders in recent years: Steve Plater, Gary Johnson and Michael Dunlop had all secured their first win before him and Ian Hutchinson was enjoying vast success, having come through the ranks at the same time. And yet Guy had led many a race, irrespective of class. So when he was asked if 2012 would finally be his year, this is what he had to say.

ABOVE: The conker fields on the approach to Ramsey have become one of the most popular vantage points at the TT. This picture of Guy in the 2011 Supersport 600cc race shows why.

" What can I say, he's my hero! I did absolutely everything I could and couldn't have wished for a better start. Those first two laps were mint but John's a wily old bugger and he gradually reeled me in. The bike was faultless and I gave it my all, but the better man won, it's as simple as that. "

GUY MARTIN ON JOHN McGUINNESS

When Guy Martin wins a TT, there'll be a national holiday.

JOHN McGUINNESS

"Well, it won't be through the lack of trying! I might not be the most talented rider in the paddock, but I'm not shy when it comes to commitment and there'll be no one more committed than me at this year's TT. I won't be riding beyond myself to try and win, but I know there's a win in me. It'll come when it's ready but it'll come – I'm sure of it."

John McGuinness perhaps summed it up best when he said, "When Guy Martin wins a TT, there'll be a national holiday." That's how big a deal it had become – and McGuinness wasn't one for exaggerating.

During the practice week for the 2012 Isle of Man TT, Martin made steady progress and the opening Superbike race saw him make a good start, lying in third place behind that man McGuinness again and Cameron Donald, who had replaced him in the Wilson Craig set-up at the beginning of 2011. He continued to hold station during the following three laps, but there was a problem with the rear wheel spindle during his final pit stop at the end of lap four, and the team was unable to replace his rear tyre.

It's common practice in a six lap race for all of the front runners to change the rear tyre at the end of the second and fourth laps, thus giving them three brand new slick tyres for two lap stints. Guy, though, had used the same rear Pirelli for four laps, leaving him at a distinct disadvantage. As a consequence of diminishing grip from a fading tyre, Guy was overtaken on corrected time by Anstey at the end of lap five, and he could only hold on to finish fourth. After the race, he said:

"On those first two laps we'd no real problems worth mentioning, but after the pit stop we had a couple of small issues that dropped us off John and Cameron's pace. By the time the rear wheel spindle caused a problem, we were out of the race for the win and I just rode it to the finish. The general handling and performance of the new GSX-R1000 is very good.

I know I can do the speeds, as we proved on that first lap and the team can do the business, so we're still in with a chance in the Senior. We've come here well prepared, but you can't test for the TT at Kirkistown or Almeria. The only place you can do that is here on the TT Course, so we can use what we learned today and apply it for Friday."

However, results at the TT were getting hard to come by for everyone, there being no less than ten potential race winners in each class, and, like everyone else, Guy was

OPPOSITE: Deep in thought. Guy was always looking to get the most out of the 2011 Relentless by TAS Suzuki GSXR1000.

" I really couldn't care less what people say about me not having won a TT. It pisses me off when people tell me what I should be doing. "

GUY MARTIN

finding the going tough. His only other results were fifth place in the Superstock race and eighth in the second Supersport outing – a far cry from what had been achieved 12 months before.

He was still faring better than team-mate Cummins, though, who was kept out of the action after sustaining a hand injury at the North West 200 when he was knocked off by a wayward Gary Johnson.

The last chance for a win was again the Senior, which was scheduled to take place on its traditional Friday. Adverse weather caused it to be postponed until the following day, and then the continuing poor weather led to the decision to cancel the race for the first time in its 105-year history.

Guy would have to wait another year to try and nail that elusive win. This had been an incredibly disappointing week: for the first time since 2006, he had failed to stand on a TT podium.

By this point, Guy's off-track activities had soared, all from the success of the film *TT3D: Closer to the Edge*. He was now in huge demand from the mainstream media, and with long-time friend Mark "Maeve" Davis, he renovated a narrow canal boat using Industrial Revolution methods for a six-part series on BBC television. This TV work, as well as his job as a truck fitter, his increasing mountain bike racing and his love of all things classic, was prompting people to say he was taking his eye off the racing ball. The general consensus was that if he really wanted to win a TT race, he should be focusing on just that. Naturally, Guy didn't agree with that thought.

"I don't buy into that philosophy and how I choose to live my life is up to me, it's got nothing to do with anyone else – I really couldn't care less what people say about me not having won a TT. It pisses me off when people tell me what I should be doing and give me the reasons why I haven't won. There are a lot of experts out there who think they know best, but they don't even know me, so how can they say that?

OPPOSITE: Guy feathers the brake as he enters Guthrie's Memorial on his GSXR1000 Superstock machine.

FOLLOWING PAGES: Deep in concentration as he tackles the Mountain during the 2012 TT.

> ❝ **I always go out and give 100%... If it's not meant to be, it's not meant to be, so I'll keep going back and trying until it is.** ❞

GUY MARTIN

Besides, it's not like I'm miles off a win either, is it? My lap times are very similar to anyone else's and I'm nearly always there or thereabouts, so I can't be doing too much wrong. I've just got to learn to be a bit more consistent. I always go out and give 100% so there are never any regrets and no ifs, buts or maybes. If it's not meant to be, it's not meant to be, so I'll keep going back and trying until it is."

The second half of the season was like previous seasons with good performances at both the Southern 100 and Ulster Grand Prix. At both events, he shared the wins with Michael Dunlop, who was rapidly becoming the man of the moment despite being only 23. He would go on to achieve plenty in the following seasons.

At Billown and Dundrod, though, Guy was a match for him and he brought his race season to a close winning five races at Scarborough's Gold Cup. There he got his name back on the feature trophy for the first time since 2009.

In typical Guy Martin fashion, it had been a year containing ups and downs. Now, just as he had done at Hydrex Honda, he opted to stay with the team for a third year, and again his main reasons centred around the TT.

"I had plenty of offers, but I always knew I would stay with Tyco if they wanted me," he said. "We get on well and they're the right folk for me. I'm staying with these boys because I think it's my best chance of winning a TT."

Team boss Neill added, "Guy is happy where he is and we're happy with him, so there's a strong desire to continue."

OPPOSITE: Guy exits Castletown Corner on his way to finishing second in the 2012 Southern 100 Championship race. Michael Dunlop was the winner.

8

2013–2014

TOUGH TIMES

TOUGH TIMES

The 2013 season was disappointing by Guy's high standards as he registered his lowest TT finishes for a number of years. There were successes and, before the year was out, he would make the podium at the legendary the Le Mans 24-hour endurance race.

Coming into the new season, Guy's attitude and outlook off the track appeared to have changed. He admitted that he'd looked at himself over the close season and had changed his approach. While people were still suggesting his fitness was letting him down at the TT – meaning that he led races, only to fade in the second half of the race – he himself was using the word "concentration". Rather than fitness, it was a lack of concentration at the crucial times that had been the main factor.

"People who say I'm not as fit as I could be are talking rubbish. There are no doubts in my mind about my fitness. The problem's with my concentration. That may sound strange given how hard you have to concentrate in a TT race, but I genuinely get bored and lose concentration as the race wears on. I'm alright for the first few laps, but then my mind starts to wander. Obviously I'm still concentrating – I'd be in a hedge if I wasn't – but it's not at the level it should be.

The buzz from racing at the TT is why I race motorbikes in the first place and can't be replicated anywhere, but by race week I'm getting a bit bored of doing the same thing lap after lap and going over the same bit of tarmac. And when that happens, I start thinking about all kinds of stuff rather than concentrating on the racing. It can be trivial stuff about what I'm going to have for tea or what's happening at the truck yard!

The Mountain's the worst. It's so open and everything looks similar, so there aren't any reference points or major landmarks. There's not really anything to keep my attention, so I lose a bit of interest in what I'm doing. If I'm to win, I've got to keep my focus for an entire six laps, not just a couple."

In what was rapidly becoming a recurring theme, the North West 200 was a disaster for all concerned. Only one race was held on the feature Saturday race day due to

PREVIOUS PAGES:
The start of the Mountain climb. Guy negotiates the Waterworks during the 2013 Superstock TT race.

OPPOSITE:
Spectacular as ever over Ballaugh Bridge on the 600cc Tyco Suzuki during the 2013 Monster Energy Supersport 600cc race.

torrential rain wiping out the programme. Fortunately, organizers had added some races to the schedule on Thursday evening to counteract such a problem, and in the three races that he contested Guy was never outside the Top 5. Third and fifth was the outcome in the Supersport races and fourth in the Superstock, but track time on the all-important Superbike was limited. Still, at least every rider was in the same boat.

As expected, he was on the leaderboard in all of his classes during practice week at the TT, but race week itself was poor. For the second year running, he failed to make it onto the podium, fourth being his best result in the opening Superbike race. He did lap in excess of 131mph once more in the Senior race but, such was the pace now at the TT, it was only good enough for fifth.

Out of his five races, he managed four Top 8 finishes, but he was a long way off the front and in one of the races, he was more than two minutes adrift of winner Michael Dunlop, whose four wins made him the man of the week. As expected, Guy made no excuses and pulled no punches in his assessment.

"It was a pretty shit week. I tried hard and the team tried hard and no one was to blame, it just didn't work for us this year. There's nowhere like the TT

ABOVE: Guy in a relaxed and cheerful mood before one of the 2013 Isle of Man TT races.

FOLLOWING PAGES: Guy celebrates on the podium after taking second place with his Team Suzuki GSXR N∞2 on September 22, 2013, at the Le Mans Circuit, western France.

> ❝ People who say I'm not as fit as I could be are talking rubbish... The problem's my concentration. ❞

GUY MARTIN

whilst talk's cheap, we just didn't have the time to get the big bike working well enough for me to challenge for the wins.

Nothing major went wrong. The Superbike was fast for a lap, but then it became a real handful and whilst I could still ride it, I couldn't go as quickly as the front few riders. We changed things for the Senior, but the bike was then a bit lazy and I had to really scratch to get the results I did. It was stable enough, but I had to have massive amounts of lean angle to get the bike to go where I wanted it to go.

The Suzuki has a very small window to work within and if you don't get the bike in that window, it makes my job that bit tougher. It's difficult to get it in the sweet spot. When you do, though, it's mega. We arrived at the Southern 100 with the bike that I'd finished the Senior with and with a bit more track time, we got it to where we wanted it to be and that allowed me to win the big race. I'm not saying if I'd have gone to the TT with the bike that finished the Southern I'd have won a TT, but it was certainly better."

The Southern 100 saw him get the better of Dunlop by less than half a second after a titanic battle that saw perfect conditions all around the Billown course. The outright lap record was bettered repeatedly, but it was Guy who was in front when it mattered and he reclaimed the title he had last won in 2009.

The Southern was his favourite meeting of the year, but the Ulster Grand Prix wasn't far behind: he carried the success on to Dundrod with a superb hat-trick, which included a double victory in the Superbike category. He also took the Scarborough Gold Cup for an amazing ninth time, reclaiming the outright lap record as well – but, once again, his best results came after the TT. This again prompted the question; was he doing enough racing early on in the year?

"I'm definitely sharper in the second half of the year and I can hold my hands up and say I don't do enough riding in the early part of the season. The team

❝ It was absolutely mega and the highlight of my season. Probably the best thing I've ever done. It's such a massive team event and like they say, there's no "I" in team, so to see everyone pulling together so much was mega. ❞

GUY MARTIN ON THE LE MANS 24-HOUR RACE

gave me a Superstock bike after the Southern and between then and the Ulster I did a few track days at Cadwell. I think I went about three times and did a couple of hours either in the morning or in the afternoon and, as well as riding at Armoy, it kept my hand in for sure.

I did a few bits and bobs at the beginning, half a day at Kirkistown, Cookstown and Scarborough, but the North West 200 was obviously wiped out, so it wasn't enough. There was nothing wrong with what we did and it was all worthwhile and valuable, but I need to do more riding. More riding will get me dialled in more, more bike fit and more used to the bike."

Other riders were continuing to contest the British Championships, and some, like John McGuinness and Michael Dunlop, were also now regulars in the World Endurance Championship. The famous Le Mans and Bol d'Or 24 hour races were giving riders a massive amount of track time, as well as numerous pre-season tests, and so Guy chose to contest Le Mans in the September of 2013.

His only previous appearance at the event – and indeed in this discipline of racing – had come in 2007 when he rode for a privateer team. This time, he was part of a Suzuki-backed squad. French expert Gwen Gabbiani was also in the team, so expectations were a lot higher this time around. After finishing in a superb second place, this is what he had to say:

"It was absolutely mega and the highlight of my season. Probably the best thing I've ever done. It's such a massive team event and like they say, there's no "I" in team, so to see everyone pulling together so much was mega. The team didn't speak much English and I don't speak much French, so there was a lot of jabbering away going on, but I did what I could.

It was a small team, which suited me down to the ground, and whilst I didn't set the world alight, I think I did OK and the team were happy enough. Strangely enough, I was quicker during the night than I was in daylight too."

Rival McGuinness was expressing the virtues of competing in Endurance races, insisting that it put him in good stead for the TT, but Guy himself was a bit more reserved. "The mileage on the bike is a definite help, but the Endurance is crammed into a few days. The TT is hard, as you're there for two weeks. Both races are about keeping it consistent, though, and require a lot of team effort. I don't want to let anyone down, wherever I race, and that's what can keep you going."

Plans were already in place for Guy to do more Endurance racing in 2014, and since there was only one round scheduled prior to the TT, early season British Superbike rounds were pencilled in too. Emphasizing how happy he was with TAS Racing, Guy remained with them for the season ahead – his fourth successive year and the longest spell he'd ever had with any team. The relationship, he explained, was as strong going into 2014 as it was in their first year together in 2011.

"I'm a bit strange in the way I go about things, but they "get" me. I'm rubbish with PR, press days and the like, but with TAS, there's a bit of give and take and

they understand me, what works with me, what doesn't, how to get the best out of me, etc. They're top, top boys and we have great craic and that's half the battle. I really enjoy working with them.

Philip and Hector are spot on. Hector's the man at the TT and pretty much runs the show – you don't see much of Philip – but everywhere else it's the other way round. We can all go out and have a beer together and it's never all about motorbikes. We can chat about anything and everything and I enjoy that. There's no pressure from them at any of the meetings and for the nationals, they give me the bikes and a van and let us work away. You get the best of all worlds with them.

Just as his activities away from the track had now increased in terms of both workload and popularity – he was a regular face and voice on TV and radio – so too had his racing season. Early season Nationals at Scarborough and Cookstown, against some good opposition, acted as a good shakedown for the North West 200 and, especially, the TT, and he visited the Southern 100 and Armoy too.

PREVIOUS PAGE:
Flying under the Dhu Varren railway bridge, Guy leads James Hillier during the 2013 Superstock race at the North West 200.

ABOVE: Conor Cummins, Michael Dunlop and Guy Martin in *parc ferme* after the Senior race Isle of Man TT in June 2014.

Further appearances at the Ulster Grand Prix and Scarborough Gold Cup, as well as the occasional World Endurance Championship appearances, meant that his calendar was complete. These meetings were the ones he enjoyed the most, and there were enough of them to keep him active and at the sharp end.

For 2014, Guy had a new team-mate in the shape of William Dunlop, son of the legendary Robert Dunlop. Though somewhat in the shadow of his brother Michael – who had already taken seven TT wins coming into the season – William was a formidable opponent in his own right, particularly on a Supersport bike.

The general consensus was that Guy would be faster than his team-mate in the 1000cc categories and William faster in the Supersport class. This was an ideal combination for the team, for it meant both riders could learn from each other and improve in their, relatively, weaker class.

Dunlop's team-mate at Yamaha in 2013, Conor Cummins, had changed teams for the new season to join McGuinness at Honda Racing. Bruce Anstey was mounted at Padgetts, and Kawasaki had James Hillier, Gary Johnson and Dean Harrison amongst their ranks.

Ian Hutchinson, was finally back racing full-time after suffering horrendous leg injuries at the end of 2010, and was now racing for Yamaha alongside sensational 2013 newcomer Josh Brookes.

Perhaps the most formidable rival was Michael Dunlop, who had shocked the racing world by leaving the Japanese giant Honda to ride a relatively unproven BMW. The German manufacturer had built a 1000cc machine expected to challenge, and were giving Dunlop the very best support possible. With his determined riding style sure to overcome any issues, he would now be the man to beat – particularly as McGuinness had a broken wrist.

Whatever happened, it was clear that 2014 was going to be another ultra-competitive year. Guy was still riding the Suzuki GSXR, now one of the older models on the grid, and knew he'd have to perform at his maximum. And with the previous two poor years at the TT, the pressure was really on.

With mixed weather at the North West 200, it was William who shone for the Tyco team. He won the opening Superbike race from Michael after a thrilling last lap, his first ever International big bike win – and one that served notice to Guy. Yes, the TT was always going to be his focus, but now he had a team-mate who had really stepped up his game.

Guy's best Superbike result in Ireland was fifth, but he did record a podium – in, perhaps surprisingly, the Supersport class, where he took a good second behind Alastair Seeley, who was now the dominant force around the 8.9-mile circuit. It was the only road race where Seeley competed and so, as a form guide, Guy was handily placed although the wet conditions had played into the hands of his slightly underpowered GSXR600.

Despite the mixed week, Guy was in a good position going into the TT. With four years' experience of the GSXR Suzukis now under his belt, he knew the bikes better than anyone else. Experienced engine guru Stewart Johnstone was now in his second year with the team, and it was clear every last bit of performance would be extracted from the bikes.

As expected, McGuinness' wrist injury kept him off the pace and race week would see Dunlop dominate. He took all three 1000cc races, proving that it didn't matter what manufacturer of bike he was riding, he was now the benchmark.

OPPOSITE: The 2014 season gave Guy plenty to smile about.

ABOVE: Sharing a joke with mechanic Denver Stewart prior to the 2014 North West 200.

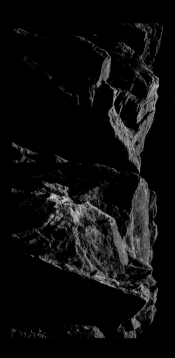

With a new lap record in each of the first two laps, Dunlop had the opening Superbike race sewn up at one-thirds distance, comfortably making up the 20-second starting deficit to Guy and circulating with him for the rest of the race. With a lap close to 131 mph, Guy took over second place and although Manxman Cummins pushed him hard, especially on the final lap, he held on for, amazingly, his seventh TT runners-up trophy.

"That was a good effort and I really enjoyed it, but I suppose it's another second place. The bike never missed a beat, but I have to take my hat off to Michael, as he's riding well," he said. "I knew Conor was catching me on the final lap and I actually thought I might have to re-pass Michael on the road and make an extra big effort."

The next three races were disappointing, though. The Superstock race ended in retirement and while team-mate Dunlop managed a podium in the second of the Supersport races, Guy wasn't competitive in the 600cc class, taking sixth and a lowly tenth despite the fact "I rode my bollocks off". A few handling issues held Guy back and his eyes were also opened by the speed of the Triumph 675, which took one of the race wins in the hands of Gary Johnson. This was duly noted for future reference.

That just left the Senior. With Michael Dunlop having dominated both the Superbike and Superstock races on his BMW and Bruce Anstey blitzing the Mountain Course with a new outright lap record in the former of 132.298 mph, the scene was well and truly set.

Conditions were again ideal on the island – but, for the second year running, Dunlop was able to make it four wins from the five races he started, for a total of 11. An opening lap of 131.668 mph meant he was never headed and left everyone else fighting for second. And in a carbon copy of the Superbike race, Guy found himself battling with Cummins for the runners-up spot.

On this occasion, it was the local hero who prevailed and Guy had to settle for third – and his fifteenth TT podium, a staggering total for someone who has never won a race. "The bike was just mint and the boys have done a great job again today. We rode a good race, which you can see by the lap times, but we have to take our hat off to Michael. That's probably the best Superbike set-up I've ever ridden around here, so yeah, I'll have to come back next year and try again, won't I," he said.

ABOVE: Guy exiting Church Bends during evening practice at the 2014 Southern 100 road races.

OPPOSITE: Guy in reflective mood following another podium at the 2014 Ulster Grand Prix

Guy went on to take the Southern 100 Championship race for the third time after seeing off the determined challenge of Dean Harrison, who had got the better of him in the earlier races that week. The Yorkshire rider had taken his maiden TT win a month earlier, and was rapidly rising up the ranks, becoming yet another rider for Guy to contend with, week in and week out.

Surprisingly, given his tally of 11 wins, he missed out on a victory at the Ulster Grand Prix although he took two more podiums. This would prove to be his final race meeting of the year as commitments away from the track kept him occupied.

By now, thoughts were already turning to the 2015 season and rumours began to circulate that TAS Racing were about to switch manufacturer. Their association with Suzuki stretched back to 2001, so it was a major decision to make for all concerned. But on the roads, it seemed clear that they were slipping behind their rivals, and a British Superbike Championship title continued to elude them.

The change came after much soul-searching from the Moneymore-based team, but it made total sense, though it brought an end to their long and happy relationship with Suzuki. The switch to the flagship BMW S1000RR would present an exciting new challenge. The team had run Suzukis for 14 years, and prior to that both the Neills had competed with Suzukis in motocross and in road racing. Philip admitted, "It was strange to be talking to another manufacturer, but also necessary. There was nothing controversial about the move but we were not where we expected to be, nor where others expected us to be."

"BMW were attractive in terms of a couple of factors: retaining our sponsors and our choice of riders for the new season. For the riders, it was clearly important to have the most competitive bikes to ensure our rider line-up. Everything came together in terms of the move to BMW and we left on the best of terms with Suzuki."

Having seen what Dunlop had done on the bike during 2014 gave Guy a terrific boost over the winter months. He would now be starting with a clean slate, It was an exciting opportunity and one he was keen to embrace.

9

2015

NEVER GIVING UP

2015
NEVER GIVING UP

In a frustrating start to the season, Guy prompted the wrath of the North West 200 race organisers when he registered his honest appraisal of the course. He was also to suffer more bad luck when attempting to achieve that elusive first TT win.

The new deal was announced in December 2014, and the official unveiling of the team's bike and colours came in February 2015. Guy would be coming into his sixteenth season of racing – and fifth with TAS – and although there were whispers of retirement, the switch to BMW and the challenge it offered gave him everything he needed to carry on.

"It's a new bike and I've never ridden it before, but we all know its pedigree. Moving to BMW machinery is the reason I'm still racing and not retiring. I'll always give it my all and to be with a quality manufacturer like BMW is mega. I'm looking forward to getting on the bikes as soon as possible.

TAS are the best team I've ever ridden for; they get me and I get them and we meet in the middle, which is why we've been successful and this new venture with BMW is just what we need going into the new season."

William Dunlop was again his team-mate, Alastair Seeley joining them at the North West 200. After testing in Spain at both Cartagena and Almeria, Guy had his first race outing on the BMW at Scarborough. There, in Superstock trim, he took his maiden win. Conditions deteriorated as the weekend wore on, but a fourth place in the second Superbike leg secured him the Spring Cup.

Following his success at Scarborough, Guy returned to the Cookstown 100, where he had his usual head-to-head battles with Michael Dunlop. There was added spice this time around as Dunlop was having his first road race outing on the Milwaukee Yamaha, but it was Guy who came out on top with a brace of Superbike victories on his Superstock machine. Dunlop pushed him close until eventually crashing out of the feature race.

Guy then got his first taste of the factory BMW S1000RR Superbike during a test day at Kirkistown in preparation for the North West 200. His arrival on the Causeway Coast generated its usual media interest – which rocketed on Thursday's second practice day when he made some controversial comments in relation to the layout of the circuit.

On return from a practice lap, Guy was briefly interviewed by BBC Sport's Stephen Watson and in a very matter of fact way, expressed his dislike of the circuit. "I'm bored to the back teeth. The chicanes have destroyed the track and my granny could go out on the

PREVIOUS PAGES: Gorse Lea just before Ballacraine is one of the most fearsome corners on the Isle of Man TT course – and the fans flock in their numbers to see their heroes in action. This is Guy on his way to fourth in the 2015 Senior TT.

OPPOSITE: Guy had his first race outing on the Tyco BMW at the Spring Cup at Oliver's Mount on April 12, 2015 in Scarborough.

> ❝ I have a lot of time for Guy, he's one of the sport's characters. But in this instance he was wrong on every level. ❞

PHILLIP MCCALLEN

BMW and ride it. The fast, big balls corners have all gone and I can't wait to get to the TT."

The chicanes had been gradually added over the years in an effort to improve safety and the total now stood at five, the latest of which was added at Mather's Cross in 2010. Given the fact that Guy had said on his debut in 2004 that he wasn't the biggest fan of the course, preferring flat-out real road racing corners as opposed to purpose built, short-circuit corners, his comments shouldn't have come as a particular surprise.

However, his outburst led to a backlash, his comments sending social media and tongues into overdrive, the majority disagreeing with him. Phillip McCallen, an 11-times winner at both the North West 200 and TT, was one such critic and was particularly vocal in his views.

"I have a lot of time for Guy, he's one of the sport's characters," said McCallen. "But in this instance he was wrong on every level with his timing and with his assertions. He'd been out there giving it his all as he chases that elusive first win and was still ten seconds off the pace. He needs to ask himself why that is instead of blaming the track. A track is a track and presents the same challenge to everyone and while there are no chicanes at the TT he's never won there either."

Needless to say, the organizers were not best pleased either, but Event Organiser Mervyn Whyte preferred not to speak openly about the matter and instead spoke in private to Philip and Hector Neill. Philip told Bikesportnews.com: "Guy knows he was wrong, although he said it was not meant in any way to discredit the event and has told me he will make a full apology to the organizers."

A hastily arranged and staged apology was made on the grid on race day, Guy saying he was sorry for the way the comments came out. "You stuck a microphone in my face in the heat of the moment," he told Watson. "I don't like chicanes, but I'm sorry for the way my words came out. As an event, the North West 200 is mega."

With another problematical day due to accidents and poor weather, it was another stop-start North West 200, Guy's best result being an eighth in the Superstock race. But lots of riders have mixed days, so this was no real indicator to the form guide for the TT.

OPPOSITE: Guy riding the Tyco Superstock BMW during practice at the 2015 North West 200. Guy's comments about the circuit didn't go down well.

" It's just pure bad luck and only something the TT can throw at you. "

GUY MARTIN

So, despite a distinctly average day in Ireland, Guy was quietly confident going into the TT. He was happy with the BMW and also the Smiths Racing Triumph that he would be riding in the two Supersport races. The bike had won one of the 600cc races in 2014 in the hands of Gary Johnson, and when Guy rang team boss Rebecca Smith to purchase one of the Triumph Daytona machines, a deal was soon reached to ride for the team outright.

Practice week, although primarily dry, saw the island hit sporadically by 50-60 mph winds which led to a disruption in the practice and race schedules. Ian Hutchinson was grabbing the headlines on the track, topping the Superbike leaderboard with a lap of 130+ mph, and Michael Dunlop was grabbing all the headlines off it. Sensationally he quit his Yamaha team mid-week and reverted back to the Buildbase BMW squad with whom he had been so successful with the year before.

This led to a race against time for him to be ready for Sunday's opening Superbike race, which ended in disaster on the final lap. Lying in third and just one mile from home, he crashed after hitting the fallen Scott Wilson. Fortunately, neither rider was badly injured and Dunlop was on the grid for all of his races.

Meanwhile, Guy's campaign had started with bitter disappointment. He was forced to retire after just three miles of the six-lap race when his machine cut out with a mysterious electrical problem on the run from Union Mills to Ballagarey.

His first result of the week came in the first Supersport race on Monday, when he finished fifth, but a penalty for speeding in the pit lane cost him any hopes of a podium and more bad luck followed in the following day's Superstock race. An opening lap of 130.304 mph and two further efforts of 129 mph should have been good enough to give him his first podium of the week, but the battery on the Tyco BMW over-heated. Despite entering his pit at the end of lap two just 5.5 seconds off the lead, Guy then struggled with his machine, which initially refused to re-start. The 35 seconds lost in the pits forced him down the running order and he eventually finished seventh.

"It was hard work out there today and even though we maybe didn't quite have the perfect set-up, I made a strong start and the bike was flying; it was mint. 130mph from a standing start is a good enough first Superbike lap, never mind on a Stocker, and the second lap wasn't much slower. We were in the running today, but what can you do. It's just pure bad luck and only something the TT can throw at you."

OPPOSITE: With BMW having no Supersport 600cc machine, Guy switched to the Smiths Racing 675cc Triumph. Seen here in action at an early season 2015 British Championship meeting.

With a relentless schedule, Wednesday was the fourth consecutive race day. Guy was back on the Smiths Triumph as well as deputizing in the TT Zero race for electric-powered bikes on behalf of injured team-mate William Dunlop, who had crashed in a practice session on Monday. Guy took fourth in the latter, and although impressed by the technology of the Victory Racing machine, he wasn't overly enamoured by the slower speeds (even if he did get round at close to 110 mph). The second Supersport race did finally give a podium finish, though.

Ian Hutchinson would take his third win of the week, just reward for the trials and tribulations he'd been through over the years, but when he came past Guy – having started ten seconds behind him – the Triumph tucked in behind and duly took third place for, amazingly, his sixteenth TT podium to date.

"The bike worked a treat and to be fair, it's better than the third place I gave it," he said afterwards. "I can't fault the team at all and when 'Hutchy' came past me, I tried to hang on to him, but he's riding so well. He started to pull away from me and was riding brilliantly,

ABOVE: Guy chatting prior to racing in the 2015 North West 200. His best finish on the day was a relatively lowly eighth.

" I could see I was in third, so rode my own race and just concentrated on securing the podium place. "

GUY MARTIN ON THE 2015 TT

so I just started to ride to my boards. I could see I was in third, so rode my own race and just concentrated on securing the podium place."

In a scenario reminiscent of years gone by, the Senior would again represent his last chance of success and after an accident halted the original six lap race, it was re-run over four laps. A disastrous start saw Guy lying in thirteenth place at Glen Helen on the opening lap – and as anyone who was at the 2015 TT will tell you, you simply cannot afford to give away such a margin. The pace at the TT now is so fast, and the competition so intense, that it really is the case that every second, and every yard, counts.

To his credit, Guy gradually clawed his way up the leaderboard. In what proved to be a sensational race, he became the fourth fastest rider in the history of the event with a second lap of 132.398 mph, also setting the quickest ever sector time from the Bungalow to Cronk ny Mona. That lap should have given him another podium at least, but that man McGuinness again proved to be master of the Mountain Course, securing victory and a new outright lap record of 132.701 mph. Guy had to settle for fourth, James Hillier and Hutchinson placing second and third.

"I was with Hutchy on the road and thought he was challenging for the win, which possibly cost me a good shot at third place, as I didn't want to start dicing with him and messing up his race. But no excuses, we were beaten on the day by the better man, but my bike was just mint. There are places we could improve, of course, but from Ramsey to the start-finish – there wasn't a better bike on the circuit."

With another TT over, Guy's twelfth in total, he was left to ponder what might have been. Whether it's fate or destiny, or pure bad luck, a TT win had failed to materialize. When it comes to the greatest road race of them all, it seems as if the gods are against him.

Naturally, his popularity was as strong and as high as ever, and only time will tell if he returns in 2016. That's something only Guy himself knows, but he's quick enough to win and the sport needs his talent and personality. A grid without Guy Martin would be poorer – of that there is no doubt.

10

AWAY FROM THE TRACK

Guy Martin has had an impact that extends far beyond that of road racing. Propelled to media stardom by the documentary TT3D: Closer to the Edge, *he has a warmth of personality that has struck a chord with the general public and has seen him host his own shows while sharing his passion for engineering.*

It's fair to say Guy's life away from the track differs from the life of any other motorbike racer in the UK, and he's now become a familiar face to many households up and down the country. The popularity of the documentary film *TT3D: Closer to the Edge* not only did wonders for the Isle of Man but also gave Guy something he never dreamed of: a career in television.

TT3D: Closer to the Edge explored what motivates the riders who race the TT, risking everything to win or just simply to compete – riders like Guy but also those throughout the grid. The film is a story about freedom of choice and the strength of the human spirit and it followed a number of riders in the 2010 race meeting, in particular Martin, John McGuinness and Ian Hutchinson. Films have been made before about motorcycle racing, as well as the TT, but none have told the story so skilfully, comprehensively or as passionately.

The end product saw Guy feature most heavily and the film then went stratospheric. Released in 2011, it was critically acclaimed in all quarters, was nominated for a BAFTA and, perhaps most importantly, was a resounding financial success – not least in the United Kingdom, where it grossed $2 million to become the seventh highest-grossing documentary of all time. Celebrities such as Chris Evans regularly tweeted about it and stars from other sports were equally vocal in their praise and admiration, not least Sir Jackie Stewart and Frank Williams.

However, the film's biggest impact was the way in which the film opened up the sport to those previously unaware of it. The TT was already enjoying a bit of a renaissance in its popularity, but the film gave it an incredible shot in the arm and spectator figures, both in terms of live attendances and television figures, rocketed. There was now a genuine appreciation, warmth and admiration for what these riders did.

The film also made Guy a star, his character grabbing the attention of all the viewers – in particular, those who had previously known nothing about the TT or motorcycle racing.

"I don't think any of us involved with the TT film had any idea of how big it would be, the response and reaction after it came out was huge," said Guy in an interview in *Bikesport*

PREVIOUS PAGES: Guy enjoys a few moments of peace and quiet at the 2015 Isle of Man TT.

OPPOSITE: The legendary sideburns receive some due care and attention.

News in 2013. "I was shocked at how big it all got. I wasn't ready in the slightest for all the attention and I'll be the first to admit I struggled with it and didn't handle it well. Things did get manic for a while without doubt."

This, though, was only just the start in terms of the attention Guy would receive as his fan base soared. North One Television produce, amongst other things, ITV4's ground-breaking coverage of the Isle of Man TT Races, and they now saw a niche in the market which, they felt, Guy could fill. Subsequently, the idea was pitched that he would become a front man of television programmes focusing on his passions for speed, engineering and motor vehicles. Needless to say, Guy had never done any television presenting before and he initially took part in some screen tests with established presenters. The idea was that a two-person presenting format would see the professional take the lead and Guy follow, easing him into this unfamiliar world.

However, it soon became apparent that the format would work best with Guy fronting on his own, enabling his personality to come to the fore without any restraints or shackles. He was likened to a modern-day Fred Dibnah in some quarters after the first programme, *The Boat that Guy Built*, was screened on BBC1. This followed Guy and his friend Mark Davis as they travelled along the canal network renovating a narrow boat called *Reckless*. Using inventions of the Industrial Revolution, the programme reconstructed early industrial processes and then used these to modernize the boat.

The programme was an unqualified success, and from that moment on, Guy's life changed – to the extent that many a chat around the water cooler in the office or factory will be about Guy Martin the TV presenter, not Guy Martin the motorbike racer.

The next series, *How Britain Worked*, followed a similar theme, with Guy presenting on his own but again focusing on engineering projects from the Industrial Revolution. Broadcast this time on Channel 4, where he's remained ever since, Guy was in his element as he embraced everything that was placed in front of him – whether it was going down a coal mine or repairing railway sleepers.

As enjoyable and fascinating as making the programmes was, their workload meant that they were also impacting heavily on Guy's life. One 30-minute episode of *The Boat That Guy*

ABOVE: Life for a motorcycle racer isn't always glamorous and there is plenty of downtime when all you do is wait.

Built could take more than a week to film – or, to put it another way, just five minutes of material for broadcast took a full day to film.

As a result, Guy and the TV producers started discussions whereby he would film and present a programme where his passion and interest were at a maximum and the disruption to his daily life at a minimum. In other words, he'd be involved only in the projects that really appealed to him.

As a result, the next programmes would follow Guy pursuing something he was totally at home with, and excited by – speed. In the 2013 programmes, he attempted to break four speed records, the first of which was the British and Commonwealth motor-paced cycling record. This involved Guy pedalling at a speed of 112.94 mph less than a foot behind a modified racing truck along Pendine Sands. Whilst he's used to going a lot quicker at the North West 200 and TT, he admitted this was one of the scariest things he'd ever done!

The next two record attempts – riding a motorcycle on the surface of water and flying using muscle power alone – proved unsuccessful, but the series ended on a high when he set a new world sledge speed record, plummeting down the Pista Riberal ski slope in the Pyrenees at a speed of 83.5 mph, and beating the previous record by over 21 mph.

Guy's enthusiasm in each project he undertook was plain to see; to say he threw himself into everything with 100% commitment would be an understatement. This served him well, not only with the people he was working with but also with the general public, who were rapidly warming to this happy-go-lucky, have-a-go character. Coupled with the fact that he always talked at nothing less than 100 mph in his broad Lincolnshire accent, complete with random expressions, wit and wisdom, he made an inspired choice for TV. He was also a natural in front of the camera, entertaining to the extreme and highly, highly popular.

Guy readily admits that he's sometimes found the media attention difficult to deal with. Indeed, some critics say it's distracted him from his racing and prevented him from winning races. That's not something he goes along with – partly because, as anyone who knows him will say, he's not the person to sit still and do just one thing.

"I'll admit there was a time when the TV stuff got a bit much and at the 2010 TT it was a real cauldron-type atmosphere with the cameras following me everywhere, but I've got the balance right now. I choose to live my life how I want and I like having more than one string to my bow. If I just had one focus in life, I'd be bored, so the variety suits me and is how I've chosen to live my life. That's my choice.

Everyone's different and I've never been the type of person who can just do one thing, I get restless. I need a lot going on to keep me occupied and if I didn't have all these things to do, I'd be a very different person and life would be a lot duller."

A second series of *Speed*, which included more record-breaking attempts, was broadcast in November 2014 and sandwiched in-between were four short episodes about Guy's *Passion for Life*. These gave an insight into the man himself and took a look at some of his hobbies, which included him showing off one of his prized possessions – a Rolls Royce Merlin engine.

The programme showed Guy firing the engine into life in a field in accordance with all the correct health and safety procedures. Doing the same at work on one occasion had proved to be one of his less inspired ideas: the power of the engine saw it get slightly out of control and destroy half of the workshop!

Guy also joined in a two-year restoration of a Spitfire that had been buried in a French beach for decades. At the same time, he told the story of its pilot, Squadron Leader Geoffrey Stephenson. In a touching finale, and with the project complete, Guy unveiled the resplendent Spitfire to Stephenson's daughters.

The most recent project, *Our Guy in India*, saw him embarking on a fascinating 1000-mile motorbike trip, as he explored rarely seen aspects of modern India en route to Rider Mania, an event described as "one of the world's maddest bike races". The production of the Royal Enfield motorcycle featured alongside tea plantations, an area close to Guy's heart; drinking up to 20 cups of tea a day isn't unusual in the world of Guy Martin, and his knowledge and taste buds for the subject reach far and wide.

Such has been the growth in his popularity and success that in mid-2015 he was linked with co-presenting the new-look *Top Gear* – another illustration of his unbelievable rise up the TV ladder. The programmes he's been involved in have certainly enriched his life even though the adulation he now receives sits uncomfortably on his shoulders – at events like the TT he simply cannot move as the public seek to get an autograph or picture or simply get a glimpse of him. Still, he fully recognizes and appreciates the chances and opportunities he's been given.

"Now I have more options in life and when I'm doing one of them, it's escapism from the other three. When I'm on the trucks, I can look forward to the TT and vice versa. I can enjoy my racing more, but as much as I love riding my motorbikes, there is more to life and I'm fortunate now to have lots of other things to do.

Yes, it can be hard trying to fit everything in, but at the end of the day, a lot of people would give their right arm to be in my position and I'd be a fool to turn down such opportunities. Like I say, I've got a good balance between everything and nothing interferes with anything else."

But it's not all about racing motorbikes and making TV shows for Guy. His love of all things mechanical, particularly trucks, has played a huge part in his life and despite his busy lifestyle and commitments elsewhere, he still works as a fitter for Moody International, a company based in Grimsby.

It all started from a young age when both he and younger brother Stuart accompanied their dad Ian to the family business, a haulage repair firm in the Lincolnshire town of Caistor. The two brothers would both become an integral part of the family business, and once Guy had completed his apprenticeship, his second home would be at the yard of Ian Martin Motor Engineers.

It was here where his engineering knowledge was shaped – not just on trucks, but on all things with an engine. Later, he would go on to prepare engines for fellow riders, some of whom would be battling with him for a win. He also learnt about precision and pride, and he sticks to both today. No stone is left unturned or corner cut, no matter what the task in hand – even if it's just mowing the lawn.

Talk to Guy about any subject on engineering, and he'll be able to hold court with you, more often than not knowing more himself than the person who started the conversation. His pride in his "Snap On" toolbox is legendary, and when I once described some cylinder heads he was porting as "a lump of metal", he promptly told me to wash my mouth out. My blunt description was blasphemy in Guy's eyes!

Soaking information up like the proverbial sponge, Guy has a tremendous breadth of knowledge about the subjects that interest him. If he comes across something unfamiliar, he'll listen intently and ask questions with an inquisitive and genuine nature, logging all the answers for future reference.

His other passion is mountain bike racing. What started out as a hobby around ten years ago has now taken on a competitive edge as he regularly contests endurance events, primarily 24-hour races, up and down the country. He's no mug either: he has finished as high as second in British Championship events and he thinks nothing about cycling 25 miles to and from work each day.

I'm proud to be able to call Guy a good friend, and the most refreshing aspect about him is that he's still the same person now as he was in 2003 when our paths first crossed. A friendship that started then is still as strong today. All that's changed is that he's a little older and a little wiser: the Guy Martin you see on television is the same as the Guy Martin in real life.

There's no pretence, no fake characteristics and no hidden agendas: what you see is what you get. In his own words, he has "arms and legs like everyone else", and that attitude is what ultimately endears him to everyone. He's a colourful yet humble and down to earth character who's simply living life to the full.

CAREER HIGHLIGHTS

CAREER HIGHLIGHTS

2003 – Team Racing

International Scarborough Gold Cup	1st
Cock o' the North Trophy, Scarborough	1st
Irish Senior Support Road Race Championship	1st

2004 – Uel Duncan Racing

Isle of Man TT, Senior	7th
(first newcomer to lap at more than 120mph)	
International Scarborough Gold Cup	1st

2005 – Uel Duncan Racing

Spring Cup, Scarborough	1st
Isle of Man TT, Senior	3rd
Southern 100 Solo Championship	2nd
Cock o' the North Trophy, Scarborough	1st
Ulster Grand Prix Superbike	2nd
Ulster Grand Prix Superstock	3rd
International Scarborough Gold Cup	1st

2006 – AIM Racing

Southern 100 Solo Championship	2nd
Cock o' the North Trophy, Scarborough	3rd
Ulster Grand Prix Superbike	1st and 1st
(first rider to officially lap Dundrod at more than 130mph)	
Ulster Grand Prix Supersport 600cc	1st and 1st
Ulster Grand Prix Superstock	2nd
International Scarborough Gold Cup	1st

2007 – Hydrex Honda

North West 200 Superbike	2nd
North West 200 Supersport 600cc	3rd
North West 200 Superstock	3rd
Isle of Man TT, Superbike	2nd
Isle of Man TT, Supersport 600cc	3rd
Isle of Man TT, Senior	2nd
Southern 100 Solo Championship	2nd
Cock o' the North Trophy, Scarborough	1st
Ulster Grand Prix Superbike	2nd
Ulster Grand Prix Supersport 600cc	1st
International Scarborough Gold Cup	1st

2008 - Bike Animal Hydrex Honda

North West 200 Superbike	2nd
Isle of Man TT, Superstock	3rd
International Scarborough Gold Cup	1st

2009 – Hydrex Honda

Spring Cup, Scarborough	2nd
Isle of Man TT, Superbike	3rd
Isle of Man TT, Supersport 600cc race one	2nd
Isle of Man TT, Superstock	2nd
Southern 100 Solo Championship	1st
Ulster Grand Prix Superbike	1st and 3rd
International Scarborough Gold Cup	1st

2010 – Wilson Craig Racing

Isle of Man TT, Supersport 600cc race one	2nd

2011 – relentless by TAS Suzuki

Isle of Man TT, Supersport 600cc race one	3rd
Isle of Man TT, Superstock	3rd
Isle of Man TT, Supersport 600cc race two	3rd
Isle of Man TT, Senior	2nd
Southern 100 Solo Championship	2nd
Ulster Grand Prix Superbike	1st and 2nd
Ulster Grand Prix Superstock	2nd

2012 – Tyco Suzuki

Southern 100 Solo Championship	2nd
Ulster Grand Prix Superbike 1st and	2nd
Ulster Grand Prix Superstock	3rd
International Scarborough Gold Cup	1st

2013 – Tyco Suzuki

Spring Cup, Scarborough	1st
North West 200 Supersport 600cc	3rd
Southern 100 Solo Championship	1st
Ulster Grand Prix Superbike	1st and 1st
Ulster Grand Prix Supersport 600cc	1st
International Scarborough Gold Cup	2nd

2014 – Tyco Suzuki

Spring Cup, Scarborough	1st
North West 200 Supersport 600cc	2nd
Isle of Man TT, Superbike	2nd
Isle of Man TT, Senior	3rd
Southern 100 Solo Championship	1st
Ulster Grand Prix Superbike	2nd
Ulster Grand Prix Supersport 600cc	3rd

2015 – Tyco BMW and Smiths Racing Triumph

Spring Cup, Scarborough	1st
Isle of Man TT, Supersport 600cc race two	3rd

Fastest Laps

Isle of Man TT Fastest lap - 132.398mph, 2015 – 4th fastest of all time

Ulster Grand Prix Fastest lap - 133.527mph, 2010 – 2nd fastest of all time

North West 200 Fastest lap – 120.932mph, 2014 – 12th fastest of all time

Southern 100 Fastest lap - 114.464mph, 2014 – 2nd fastest of all time

Scarborough Fastest lap - 83.898mph, 2013 – outright lap record holder

PREVIOUS PAGES: A third place in the Supersport 600cc race at the 2015 Isle of Man TT gave Guy his 16th podium at the event. Here he sweeps round the iconic Creg ny Baa.

FOLLOWING PAGES: Dropping down Deer's Leap at the 2014 Ulster Grand Prix – road racing at its best.

PICTURE CREDITS

❝ A lot of people would give their right arm to be in my position and I'd be a fool to turn down such opportunities. ❞

GUY MARTIN

The publishers would like to thank the following sources for their kind permission to reproduce the pictures in this book.

Alamy: /Michael Conway: 64-65; /WENN Ltd: 104

Gavan Caldwell: 149, 153, 154-155

Clive Challinor: 60, 69, 71, 112, 143

Dave Collister: 27, 32-33, 36-37, 42-43, 45, 49, 50, 55, 91, 136-137

Corbis: /Sutton Images: 59, 62

www.diegomola.com: /Diego Mola: 80-81, 100-101, 129, 133, 135, 140, 144, 158-159

Fotolibra: /Geoff Lipscombe: 66

FoTTofinders: 15, 24-25, 70, 72-73, 78, 83, 88-89, 94, 96, 103, 108-109, 120-121

Getty Images: /Hagen Hopkins: 6-7, 10, 132; /Jean-Francois Monier/AFP: 126-127; /Richard Sellers: 139

Gold & Goose Photography: 104

Tony Goldsmith: 9, 77, 82, 85, 97, 110, 115, 146-147

Pitlane Photography: /Martyn Wilson: 124

Press Association Images: /Barry Coombs: 52-53

Rex: /Julian Makey: 130-131; /Moviestore: 150

Topfoto: /Tim Williams/Actionplus: 123

WPFotos: /Peter Faragher: 4, 63, 86, 98, 106, 116-117, 119, 134

Phil Wain: 12-13, 16, 18, 20-21, 23, 28, 30, 35, 39, 41, 46, 75, 92

Every effort has been made to acknowledge correctly and contact the source and/or copyright holder of each picture and Carlton Books Limited apologizes for any unintentional errors or omissions that will be corrected in future editions of this book.

The author would like to thank Guy Martin, Matt Lowing for being the driving force behind the project; Paul Phillips for all his advice and feedback in writing the book; David Miller, Larry Carter, Gary Pinchin, Michael Guy, Paul Lindsay and Malcolm Wheeler for believing in me and for giving me opportunities over the years; and finally to all my friends and family for their continued love and support.